MW01598753

WE THREE
Go South

The 1890 Diary of Ethel Richardson's
trip to the Sub-Antarctic

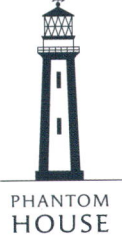

PHANTOM
HOUSE

Acknowledgements

First and foremost I wish to thank my family for
encouraging me throughout this project.

Thank you Grant Sheehan, for recognising the merit
in producing this story, the wonderful photography of the
subject matter and the wise advice given.

To Michael Browne who knew Ethel when he was a child and
became my esteemed friend through seeing one of "Fluff's"
paintings in my house, thank you for filling in the story.

And thank you to the three Victorian "tomboys"
for leaving me such a wonderful account of their trip.
It has enriched my life.

Designed by typeface ltd. www.typeface.co.nz

Printed in China by Toppan Leefung Printing Ltd.

First published in 2014 by Phantom House Books Ltd ©
PO Box 6385 Marion Square, Wellington, New Zealand

E-mail info@phantomhouse.com www.phantomhouse.com

ISBN 978 0 9876667 8 9

Ethel Richardson

Prologue

Some seventy years ago, as a small child, one of the best incentives I could be offered to eat up dry mashed potatoes and spinach at dinnertime, was an opportunity to look at "Aunty Fluff's" sketch book. This rickety old book, with a wrinkled vellum cover falling apart at the spine, illustrated the memories of my great aunt's trips to many of the outlying islands of New Zealand and some fantasy escapades as well, which are marked "Not True".

Through these amusing sketches I grew to love the three Victorian tomboys who featured on the pages and it fostered in me a longing to see the wonderful wild places they had visited in the 1890s. The trio were the daughters of George and Augusta Richardson who raised a family of five including two sons, on a run property in Southland called "Oaklands". Their seafaring tendencies were probably instilled by their mother, who was the granddaughter of an Admiral in the British navy.

Lillie, the eldest of the three girls, was to become my grandmother but died before I was born. The youngest, Aunt Fannie, once dubbed by an admirer "the most vivacious young woman in Wellington" was the only one I knew personally because she lived close enough to be a regular visitor to our farm in Pahiatua. When I was little she taught me many of the rudiments of watercolour painting and through her I gained an insight into the essence of these extraordinary young women.

In 1890, the family was living at the ministerial residence in Tinakori Road Wellington as George Frederick Richardson, their father, had become member for Matura and Minister of Lands and Mines in the Atkinson government. It seems that the girls – by then aged 19 to 23 – were extremely emancipated for the era and their parents were quite willing to allow them to go unchaperoned on the government steamship Hinemoa to visit the Sub Antarctic Islands where the ship was servicing lighthouses and establishing depots for survivors of possible shipwrecks.

Fanny Richardson

Captain Fairchild, on the Hinemoa, must have been an indulgent friend of the family to have taken on responsibility for these high spirited girls as they mercilessly teased the young sailors on board and embarked on numerous wild adventures. He was, however, no stranger to their ways as they had already done a circumnavigation of New Zealand and visited the far-flung Antipodes, Chatham and Kermadec Islands. In contrast with their age group today, the girls created fun from very simple things and romantic experiences, although present as an undercurrent, were muted.

Many years later, I inherited, amongst other mementoes, a dairy written by Ethel (Aunty Fluff) of the 1890 trip south. Suddenly the enchanting old drawings became even more significant in acquainting me with a grandmother and great aunt I had never known and I realised the significance their story has in telling a unique version of what our Sub Antarctic islands were like at the time. It was over 100 years later that I made the journey myself and fully appreciated what they had so blithely undertaken.

It is difficult to imagine today: making the decision to embark on a six week voyage to the Southern Ocean on the toss of a coin, with only half a day to prepare and that the most important things to be purchased prior to leaving were violin strings and Eno's fruit salts. Today we have thermal underwear, Gortex jackets, neoprene boots, GPS and satellite phones, but they had only their long skirts, high buttoned boots, ulsters and gamps to protect them from the freezing conditions. It makes an enchanting tale which in spite of the dire warnings in the opening pages of the diary, I now share with you, bad spelling and all, just as she wrote it.

Cynthia Cass

This, my six weeks log, is not meant for all hands and the cook to look at, but only me and mine now do you see!

This was copied into this book some years after from the rough sheets I wrote at the time, I had a very good mind to alter some of the words when I came to them – but no, I thought I'll leave them, good bad or indifferent, as they were then so shall they be now, – raddical rude wretches we were too. Never-the-less it was us – O! tell tale log!! To tell of all our wickedness & of little good (or none) – that brings back old times, some forgotten – some well remembered – never to be forgotten while our memory shall remain – and to tell of others actions in far vanished years –and dear old friends among them – that have scattered since and wandered, far away – far away. "Who knows when we shall meet, or if we'll meet again" – there is much to be read between the lines on these pages, who'll read that? no one, but we three.

Friday
26th September 1890

> *Us three desided at dinner time we would go the South trip.*

But before that we were so nearly going, that Fannie and I went flying off down town to get fiddle strings, and Fannie got a hat, and then we went and saw Captain, and he said, we would have "a week at the Bluff", (just what we wanted so we could see dear little old Lizzie again) I told him we weren't desided, and he said "come", that turned the point so we flew off home at the rate of knotts to tell Lillie, and the "Hinemoa" was to sail at 3, and we had nothing ready.

When we got home it was just dinner time, and we told Lillie Captain said (come) and we'd have (a week at the bluff) and that he was all in a good mood over it, and seemed to want us to come. Lillie said while we were away "Dan Moran" came to give us our music lesson and started playing tunes to let us know he was waiting, and Lillie was not game to go and tell him we were out, ("Yes, yes, yes! very wrong of sisters to miss their lesson.") Lillie put all her precious old ferns out of the drawing room into the hot house so they would'nt die for want of water.

Lillie & I & Fannie, in the days of our youth.

9

In the morning I had wanted to go, and Lillie and Fannie were undesided, so I said we'll toss for it...

I got a 2 shilling bit and it came out we wouldn't go, so we said we would just for spite, and to prove the coin false ("in which the widow Wanderslosh proves false to the pat of butter") or the tail of her coat.

Fannie didn't want any one to go routing in her paper drawer, so she wrote on a bit of paper ("any one who dares to go at my drawer has a darned good cheek, except Pa, he often goes to it for pens and things").

We got our box packed, and Kennerly came up for our baggage so we said good bye to Ma (a little manning of the pumps over it). I hate saying good-bye – down we went leaving Ma and the boys, I mean King and Harry came with us, and Harry got out at Barauds the chemist and got us a bottle of Eno's fizz and some sticking plaster, Ma said we were to get. We posted a letter to "B.T." to tell her to go and see Ma. We found the "Hinemoa" was at the Queens Wharf alongside a coal hulk next the "Wanaka". Mr. Neale put our baggage on board, and told us they were leaving at 5. We saw Nina F there, an awful masher. We said good-bye to King and Harry, and King promised to look after "Imey" for me, and to water my pansies, poor little "Imey" I hated leaving her. Then we went round to the "Orari", she was right opposite the "Hinemoa", to say good bye to Bilton and Ernest, first thing we saw was Bilton flying over the gangway in blue pants with a paint pot in one hand. A man with more brains than most came up and asked "if we wanted to see anyone?" We told him Ernest, so he went and found him and sent him to us, and Lillie gave him the flowers, we saw the cabin after all, and Bilton blue pants and all. Then we went off up to "Black Top" and she gave us a cup of tea and some bread and butter. Jack was there (bother him) and an old owl of a woman was in the kitchen too, so we had our tea and stuff in the scullery, then we said farewell to dear old "BlackTop' and she wished us all the good luck in the world. Off we went down to the railway wharf and met Mr. Neale, he told us he wasn't coming, he stopped for the "Stella" worse luck. Ernest came round to see us off, and we went on board, and saw Nina and Edith with Capt. Sargent and some other girls on the "Pleione", showing off 19 to the dozen.

It was just 10 minutes past 5 when we left, little Gore was on board and old Hislop, and Gore's mate, and a sort of 2nd "Adigo", and a whole lot more scarecrows, all bound for Lyttelton only, and a good job too. We had a fair wind and a fine day for a start, N W breeze, we had my cabin and Lillie and Fannie had my old one I had round the North trip.

Lillie feels the water with her toe to see if it is too cold, and —

We passed the "Kinmore" barque, outside the heads, 102 days from Liverpool, the Mana was towing her in, it was middling cold out side and not a bit nice. We had tea in the straits, and after tea we 3 sat on the settee and watched some of the others having their tea, a constabulary man and "Rum and 'oney" who had awful eyes and rolled them about all the time, and a mouth which he kept chock-a-block the whole time, and only stopped stowing for a small space to tell how rum and honey ('oney) was good for a cold (hence his name), and he talked of his 'oses, and said "o, was yer?", "aint" and "ave" and all sorts of things, and Lillie said he sucked, and clicked, and clacked like a baboon, and grinned from ear to ear – poor man how mean of us to sit taking him in all the time, but good luck to him all the same. Lillie said the constabulary man's one ear stuck out more than the other, from always ballancing his cap on it. We were very sleepy so we turned in at 8 and got to Lyttelton on...

Saturday
27th September 1890, 9am

*It was a fine morning
and we had breakfast just
as we were coming into harbour,
our passengers all went by
the first train, good thing too.*

Slips in. ("Maitai River".) Nelson.

We passed the old "Wairoa" as we came up, anchored out. We stayed on board for a bit to watch the horses go ashore, "Rum and 'oney" was in agony when the horses were coming up out of the hold, lest they should get skinned, he said "don't let the box touch the mares' quarters" "hold on, you've got it right against 'er foot", "mind their 'eads, don't let their 'eads touch coming up". We went along to see the 4 masters "Silverhorn" and "Knight of St. Michal" with Captain and he took us on the "St. Michal", we wanted to go on the "Silverhorn" but they wouldn't let us. Captain told us the "Devonport cost them 3000 to build", he took us on the brigantine "Nettie", she had been burnt a few days before.

Before dinner us 3 went to the baths, Fannie and I had a swim, or tried to, I told two little boys to go away as I wanted to have a splash, not they, so I said "go away you kids!" and one said "will I!" so I splashed them, (but not they,) then Fannie said "little boy will you go away from here please, this is the time for girls to bathe, and if a policeman catches you here, he'll walk you off". After a bit they both went. Lillie sat and laughed at us the whole time, no wonder, the bathing dresses we had on were so big they were nearly dropping off us, and the arm holes were big enough to walk through. We were the first of the season to have a swim (so the woman said) and it was rather cold too. All the fence was broken away, I suppose that was to let the sharks in, to try and eat us. ("If you're meant to be gobbled up, you will be gobbled up.") We had a shower of fresh water when we got out, got dressed and made tracks back again and went and got a brush and comb (we left ours behind in our hurry coming away) the brush had Kent and Sons on it, and the man said the comb was "real horn" and "the brush by the *best maker in the world*" we gave 5/ – for the two, which nearly ruined us, we didn't bargin for leaving our brush and comb behind.

After dinner we went round to the maori village, or pah, or kaika, or what ever you call it, it is 6 miles from the wharf, we went all through it and saw a ton of geese and heaps of little ones, a boy brooming up rubbish, and a church with the bell hung on a tree. There were a lot of maoris there, and heaps of pigs all sizes, and coming round we saw a yellow rabbit, and a poor little grey one dead, by the road, and we saw a tug taking a topsail schooner off a slip half way round. Coming back Lillie and Fannie wanted a drink and we saw a milkman going to a house just above the road so they went there, as soon as the milkman came out, (I waited on the road) they asked for some water, and *got it.*

Captain went to Ch.Ch. and we wasted all the evening, and turned in early. Just after I was in bunk a cockroach fell pat on my neck, I said *Lillie!* and hopped up, and it only went down further, I got it in the end and killed it with the heel of Lillies boot. We heard the S. A. band playing the old "Swannie" so nicely and about 10 we heard such groans and cheering when the "Wanaka" and "Te-anau" left. Lillie said Arthur was evidently taking his teeth in and out, by the sounds we heard in the pantry.

Sunday

28th September 1890

We were up early, and all the hills were so lovely with thick mist all over the tops, just like Scotland would be ("and the mist creeps o'er the mountain").

We had breakfast by our selves as Captain wasn't back, and *bad* bacon and eggs to start with. We stayed on board all morning, and all wrote to Ma, after dinner Captain took us on board the "Silverhorn", she was very nice, and they had up (no admittance except on business) but we went on just the same, they had some fruit on the table aft, in the pantry a lovely tart and some good looking curranty cake, we came back and after tea we 3 went to church. The bells only rang about 5 minutes. We got to a church and found it wasn't the english one, so asked a girl where it was, she said "round the corner". We went round and asked a man if that was it? He didn't know, he was a stranger so we went in and found it was it and just like the Oamaru church and nice inside. The man sat us down by the front to the port side, the minister rolled his eyes, and never looked at the people once, but the ceiling all the time and turned his back to the people, and we nearly had to smile. We found he was the same one Orry told us of who preached about (*the thunder bolts of Heaven*). We came back and "Moondyne" gave us some ginger cracks, that Lillie said were made out of *china*. Arthur went and screwed up our ports and Fannie told him to undo them again, and he did, turned in at 10.

Monday
29th September 1890

We woke at four a.m. the "Hinemoa" made such a row letting off steam. Lillie got up and looked out the port, all the harbour was moonlight, and mist creeping slowly round the hills.

We left early and got to Akaroa hds. about 10, didn't go up this time, sent a boatload of stuff ashore to the lighthouse. We were so close to the rocks you could almost jump ashore. Then we left for Moeraki, there was such a thick fog too, and cold, we passed a ketch. I got "Merryeanus" to get me a board from forrard and made a draft board out of it, and some cork men, that blew away when we played on deck, so we got a potato from by the galley and made men that wouldn't blow away out of the potato, we read most of the afternoon. Lillie went to sleep and I made this up and wrote it in one end of Lillie's book...

We often used to call Lillie "Billie" (so for the poetry) just for fun.

Steaming on the ocean
Through a misty vale,
The sinking glass denotes to us
A strong and vicious gale.

The rising wind scares all the fog
Many a mile away
And in a row on the deck we sit
This bright and sunny day.

A gull sits on the foremast truck
And yells to make us look
It sits there as these lines I write
In snoosing "Billies" book.

"Nimble" was at the wheel. I got two sketches to-day one of Akaroa and one of Moeraki too. It was so foggy we stopped the engins and drifted, thick thick, everywhere. We turned in at eight, early enough, but still, soon we were asleep.

"Points at Akaroa heads." Monday 29th 9/1890

16

Tuesday
30th September 1890

We are up early, it was cold and cloudy...

We were at Moeraki at daylight, finished and went on to Port Chalmers, and got there at 11 a.m. Coming from Morakei we saw such lots of mutton birds and when there we saw heaps and heaps of black swans, flying in patches all over the sky, close, and further out till you could hardly see them, and making such a funny noise.

After we had dinner we 3 went strait up to Miss Sinclair's and found no one in, so we came back down to the school, and asked for her and were waiting in a sort of passage, when we heard *clump*, *clump*, *clump* and the floor shaking, and we knew it was her by the wait, out she came, all joy to see us, and so nice again, dear old monster.!!!!

There was only one barque in, the "Ranee" with a monkey gaff. When we were up at Miss Sinclair's house we took some wallflowers knowing she would not mind, and we got a sprinkle as it came on to rain a bit. Miss Sinclair gave us a lot of flowers, and took us to Mrs. Ritchie's shop, opposite the Sailors rest, and gave us such a feast of cakes and lollies, good old soul, and made us promise to bring our violins up after tea, then we went on board and Lillie wrote to Montie and we all wrote to Ma. After T we all went up violins and all and some other old mother hubbards came poking in – a Miss Duncan and Miss Downs and Aunt Ada who was

such an owl she was afraid to go out alone in the country even in the *day-time*, great ass! and put on more side than her head was worth, some of them did anyway.

Miss Sinclair's *old* servant Jenny was as scotch as old boots, she told us all about her turkeys ("Aye! the bug 'uns and the bubbie, and all the little yuns!"). She said she was going home to Scotland in a few years, and she is as old as the hills and nearly dead now, and can hardly waddle at all. After a while the others went, and we had some nice music, only Miss Sinclair's piano was so old half the notes were dummy and Lilly could hardly play. Miss Sinclair had a very ancient violin with a lovely tone, she played for us too, and Fannie wanted her to change violins, but Miss Sinclair wouldn't. She called me "Fluffy" and "Goodie" and told me she used to when I was a wee little beggar, she said I was so good, I was always called "Goodie", its a pity to be good when you're young because look what you grow up like! *ME*!!!!!!

Miss Sinclair gave us some cocoa, and showed us a gold violin string – her house is full of fleas too – old Jenny went out in the dark and got us a lovely bunch of wallflowers and O! the scent!!! and she told us again of her pet turkeys ("O the bug bubbie and the wee hen wi the six wee chicks out") we told Miss Sinclair how the Steward always stood and stared at us when we were at meals, and we hated people to watch us eating, she said ("O! just, just – roll your eyes and eat all the more") then we made tracks for the "Hinemoa", and it was cold too.

17

TRUE.

Friday November 27/ 1891.   (Lillie Ethel & Fannie running to a fire.) 2. 25 d. m

Wednesday
1st October 1890

Roused out, a fine morning, and the "Hinemoa" not going up to Dunedin. The "Ranee" alongside loading, and the "Rotomahana" and "Ringarooma" both laid up.

We posted Montie's letter and found out about the trains and came back for Fannie's cash, and off we went at 10 minutes past 9. The train was so full we had to stand on the platform. It came on to rain and we were on the weather end of the carriage, and got christened again. A jolly rude man tugged open the door when I had my hand on the handle and tore my glove that Fannie and I got at Te Aro, and hurt my hand too. *Clown!* When he came out we all gave him such a look, great owl!

When we got to Dunedin we went strait to the wharf to look at the ships, the "Jessie Readman" was there and 2 barques "Clan Macleod" and "Langstone" and the "Catlin" and "Comet" and "Edith May" with a green hull. Next we went and telegraphed Lizzie, to tell her we were coming, *and to come*, then we went to a shop and got a silk scarf and a box of handkerchiefs for her and got we some fruit for Mrs. Kydd and took the tram out to her. Jessie saw us coming up the hill and came to the gate to meet us, we saw Mr. and Mrs. Kydd and Nellie, and Lizzie was there with Ruby, she is only the size of a big pin and says "bless her heart" to her doll and says "O! no" if they ask her if she likes pepper?

We stayed for dinner, we had boiled fowl (that was hatched before the ark) but we enjoyed it very much as we were hungry, and sago pudding. Nellie and Jessie came out and helped me get some of those wee little pansys, they were growing under a goosbery tree, and had such dear wee faces, Mrs. Kydd gave us such a heavenly drink of milk. Nellie wanted a holiday, so we went and asked, I hid Nellie with my gamp, as she didn't want to be seen and Lillie went and asked, they gave her a holiday, so off we went. Mrs. Kydd gave us our tea between 3 and 4, she wouldn't hear of us going without, (kind old good Mrs. Kydd) we left their place at 4 and went to see Agnes, she was busy so we went down Princes St.

We went to the station at 6 and left at a quater past for Port C. and got down at 7. We got a telegram from Ma, and a letter from Montie ("O! Billie Billie") is still with him on the "Zealandia", we wrote to Ma, and then practised, and didn't turn in till 11, but we were soon in the land of nod.

Thursday

2nd October 1890

We turned out early and went for a walk, we were away by seven and went all round by the water, it was very nice, and a lovely morning, we went right round the sort of perninsular.

We sat for a bit on a seat that had a big O.M.R. carved on it, viewing around ourselves. Went ashore after breakfast and took Miss Sinclair back her music book she lent us, (Allan's reels and strathspays). We were going up the road above the port where Mr. Campbell told us to go up, to get some good earth to plant my pansies in, and Miss Sinclair came part way with us, just up past the church, she showed us all the different churches, and said ("one can go to Heaven any way they like, just pay your money, and take your choice"). We departed and on up the road, got some good earth, and I got my handkerchief full. We went on up the road a wee bit and looked round the corner and back on board, just in time. We got some apples and took aboard, and passed on our way out the "Rud Josephy" and "Tieri".

We stopped and landed the stores at Tairoa heads, Captain told us of a poor little boy who was playing with a little roller and it went over a cliff and in trying to get it he fell over too. We passed a whole lot of fishing boats, all sailing in one after the other, they were going along at a good rate as they had a fair breeze, one was called "Te Koti" and one the "Maori". We finished there at dinner time and on round Cape Saunders, and got there about 3 p.m. I got a sketch.

Opposite Cape Saunders.

Cape Saunders 21.10.1890.

It was awful cold, and landed stores. Lillie and Fannie had a fight sitting by the skylight. I planted my pansies in a tin "Moondyne" got for me, it is as calm as can be just now. We were in no hurry to get to the Nuggets before daylight so sailed from here, and the engines were stopped and we did go awfully slow. "Nimble" was at the wheel and Captain scolded him for not steering properly and there was so little breeze you could scarcely keep steerage way on her, it was so smooth, just as smooth as can be, grand and calm, we were really almost only drifting.

"Nimble" had to go up and loose the sails, and we sat on the deck all afternoon, and it was so cold, we were freezing to the backbone. We started having fun sitting down on the deck, and "Merryeanus" came along and said to Fannie "mercy you're an awful little blue nose" and Fannie said "you cheeky old blue-coated old" – then she saw him and stopped. Then old Campbell came by, and Fannie said "I good dee to you!" Lillie said she was a "rude little animal" and she kept on pulling Lillie's nose and we were having such fun the Mate had to grin (although he was such a buffilde old chap) as Lillie said.

Today I found a pair of small scissors, smothered in rust, stuck down behind my chest of drawers, and after tea Fannie sent them along to "Merryeanus" and two slug-eaten pansy blossoms (off my little pansys) and a bit of paper round them with "*Love and best wishes*" on it. We practised for a bit, and Lillie and I had a fine snoose on the settee. We turned in early as it was cold, and we had nothing to do.

24

Friday
3rd October 1890

Up early and found ourselves at the Nuggets at daylight, and a big sea running. We were anchored on the North side, too rough to land. Just before dinner we hove up and went round to the South for shelter, and anchored there for the night.

Lillie felt **rather rum** and turned in at 6. Fannie and I routed out all the draws in the saloon to see what we could find, Fannie routed out the starboard cubbord and found a cookery book, she said "O! here's a cookery book"! We were just roaring laughing, as "Moondyne" was in the pantry. The "Hinemoa" is 14 years today, since she went to Wellington, in 76. It is rough and an awful big sea running. Before turning in Fannie and I thought of all the good things we could, and longed to eat them. There was such a lovely wild sunset to-night, and all the water was big slouching pink waves, and all white, white, amongst the rocks. Fannie and I turned in at a quater past 8.

25

Saturday
4th October 1890

Finds ourselves back to the North side and the sea much better and the wind down, but still a heavy surf on the beach, so could not land till eleven, it is fine, and warm now.

We steamed close in and landed before dinner two boatloads, in loading the first boat a case of paraphine slipped out of the sling, and went flying into the boat and smashed the thwart to atoms, and went bang against "Nimbles' leg and cut his finger. We left at 12 for the rivers, passed a union boat, we only steamed close to the 3 rivers and on, it was too rough for more. "Nimble" was at the lead, and he kept on heaving without calling out how many fathoms, and Captain got wild with him, and told him to "come out of that, he was no better than a fool." and started scraping out an oily mark on the bridge. Fannie and I had a fight for my book "Sam's Sweetheart" she was trying to get it from me, "Nimble" was at the wheel and had to laugh at us, so I copied him in the end of my book, and Lillie, and a fireman (she doth roll).

"Merryeanus" came past and asked us who sent the scisors? and said to Fannie "look at her blushing" and Fannie was so wild with him she said *"O! A. Knox"* she was in such a hurry to say something. It is a grand fine day now, we had "consequences" on deck, and laughed over them till we were limp, and threw them overboard after. We steamed through a swarm of mutton birds, some dived to get clear of us and some ran for bare life, in all directions, poor little beggars. We past Waipapa light house, and the old "devils bridge" and poor old Toi Tois, saw a schooner heading for there, O! a happy day this, truly, soon to see dear little old Lizzie and Pa and Ernest and most likely "Captain" too.

On we go for the Bluff – something happened to the low pressure boiler, (or silender) and the high one has to do all the work, about Waipapa they went rong, Oh! happy day come back again. Lizzie waits at the Bluff – what a day of happiness – soon to see Lizzie – then the engines go slow for a time – and off again quick! thump– thump– thump– two or three times getting slower and slower– till they stop– * * then off they go quick, thump! thump! thump! thump! thump! thump!, as if they meant to get her into the Bluff before dark, then they seem to think its no use and go slower and slower and stop –

I went down to write this and watched out the port hole and saw the land pass – and the buoys. Lillie came down for some biscuits and took as many as she could carry, and "Gilpin" saw her, (she generally sends me for them) We saw a brigentine away out by Stewarts Isd. then we got in just at dusk, about 7. And down came Lizzie like a real good brick, we saw her coming down and flew off without our hats up the wharf to meet her, we kissed her and hugged her – dear little old friend after five long years apart – she is just the same, as in our wild young days, we didn't expect to see her half so nice, or so like her old self, I thought she would be all changed and old and grumpy (but NO!) ("pleasures that come unlooked for are thrice welcome"). We each grabbed up some of her baggage, and came on board, we were all one broard grin with joy. Good little thoughtfull Lizzie! She brought us scones and half a bit of cake baked in a camp oven, she made both, and ham (poor little Lizzie) that she cured herself, and some apples and flowers from dear old "Oaklands". We sat in a corner and yarned the whole evening and ate almonds and rasons, that "Moondyne' gave us for the occasion. We turned in at 10, and Lillie and Lizzie turned in together in Lillie's big bunk, and soon we wandered together in the land of dreams, far away far away from the "Hinemoa" and the Bluff.

Sunday

5th October 1890

We woke to find Lizzie was with us, hurrah!!! boys!!!

Turned out at 7. Had a good wash as we were still, and after breakfast we went up to the Eagle hotel for Lizzie to see Mrs. Hamilton's, then Lizzie and us went for a walk to the point, we went to the pilot's house for a drink, he gave us some good water, and showed us a pencil drawing of the "Stella" over the mantlepiece done by Leighton a light house keeper at Cape Maria.

We went and sat on the beach for a bit, but had to move on as the sand flys were gobbling us wholesail, and coming back I went down a bank to get some black berrie roots for Lizzie she wanted to take some home, the broom and gorse was out lovely, we got some, and the Sun popped out, ("with a flash of light like a shower of gold on the bonnie yellow broom") it was clouding up everywhere.

⌇⌇⌇⌇⌇⌇⌇⌇⌇⌇⌇⌇

Back in good time for dinner, it came on to rain after so we stayed aboard all afternoon, Lillie showed Lizzie her dairy and Montie's letter, the sand flys are crawling all over the port holes in dozens, Lizzie got in a corner and started to read "Pomroy Abbey" lots of visitors came, about 2 dozen, and Fannie set them all singing, any that could (or squeeling its all the same) Just before tea, came "Moondyne" and beconed to me from by the pantry door I made my way out through all hands, and he told me two young gentlemen were waiting to see us, I looked up and there was "Captain" and his baby brother Charlie, who had a pinkey cap and legens on and a tag of fair hair hanging down in front, and a stock whip, so had "Captain", they stayed for tea, and after tea they and Lillie and Fannie went for a walk along the beach and stood out at the signal pole it came on to rain so they came back but did not get wet.

Lizzie and I went to the Methodist Church, the only one we could see, the preacher said about "a man with a quivering lip and a tear in his eye and singing "Home sweet home" steaming back to Tonga" and about a man that came down stairs in new clothes and said "how do I look old fellow?" and the other said "you look very well, very well indeed". There were 25 lights in the church, because I counted, and about 70 people all told. Coming out of church Lizzie and I both forgot about the steps and went sprawling down, and we followed the crowd to find our way home. "Captain" asked Lillie about "Bobstay" and she told him he was coming to Wellington, and we were awfully glad. The barque "Hesper" beat the record coming from Newcastle here she was only 4 days and 20 hours. We watched the brigentine "Cers" beating up from the heads after dinner. Fannie told Lizzie how they walked with the two Clares, and drew a picture of herself with her arm around Charlie's waist, just for fun, and Lizzie was very much shocked. Fannie went into the pantry and asked "Moondyne" for some pickles, and asked him "if he wanted any roasted biscuits, because if he did he wouldn't get any". "Captain" and Charlie went and we larked about and wrote and turned in after 10.

Monday
6th October 1890

Awake early, find ourselves steaming for Center Island, and get there at eight, and anchor, poor little Lizzie sick.

A lovely fine morning, we landed 2 boat loads of stuff, Lizzie came on deck with us in the sun, and we lent over the rail on the bridge and watched them going ashore, and yarned, Lizzie still felt rummy, but better than she was, and Fannie told her how she had to go ashore at Cuvier on the load of timber, Lizzie thought it was terrible, so Fannie told her for fun that she was even floated ashore on some timber towing after the boat, Lizzie couldn't get over it.

O! the mountains in the South did look so lovely.

We got a wee billy of milk first thing from Centre Island. At breakfast Fannie put milk into *Lillie's* glass, to make out *Lillie* had drunk it, and it was *her* all the time Then we make for Dog Island, and get there at 12. We had a practise, it is nice and calm now, Lizzie still bad, we landed the stores, and brought off a little girl to go to Gore, all by herself. "Moondyne" showed us a big stuffed kiwi, after dinner us 3 wrote to Pa, still anchored off Dog Island. Lizzie did not enjoy her trip on the briney very much it is the first time she has been on the sea (and at the Bluff) since she came out from Ireland.

We got back to the wharf at 3, and there was Ernest like a starved cat, in the cold waiting for us, it was cold too, he had been waiting for us all day, and went and perched on the hill, with a bad hedache, and sat on a tussock and watched us, and he brought us two such *lovely* bunches of pansies and "Ladies Garter" sticking out everywhere and bits of "Wallflower". Ernest stayed for tea, and O! he *did* show off, and he *is such* a fright, he has had all his moustache shaved off to act in "Mikado" and it is only half grown, and is such a sight, he chewed in all that was left of it and looked such a *perfect beast*.

Lillie and Ernest went up to telegraph to Ma, and got some lollies too, when they came back Ernest would come to our cabin to tidy himself for tea, he took *our* brush and pretended to *spit on it*, when I saw him I said *Lillie!!!* and Ernest went on brushing his hair up and kept on *Lillie!!! O! Lillie!!!!* then turned round and brushed up our hair, and roared laughing at us (*old beast!*) I said "Stop it Ernest, I wasn't touching you, Ernest". He only teased us all the more and kept on "*Ernest, I wasn't touching yer Ernest*?" "Ernest, stop it Ernest, I wasn't touching yer Ernest" when he was washing his hands we routed up his hair, and hid the

This is ment to represent the sound of a piece of sillier music.

NOT TRUE.

31

TRUE AND YET
NOT TRUE.

"Three horses riding three horses."

brush, he used the comb then, when she saw him going to get a towel to dry his hands on she grabbed up hers, so he took Lillie's and dried on it, then he took Lillie's pillow to wack us with and spied her garment underneath, Fannie and I both said *O! Lillie*!! as he pounced on it, and grabbed it up, he held it up in the air above his head, and said *O! Lillie*!! *O! Lillie*! As he was putting it back, Fannie grabbed one of her deck shoes and wacked him with it, in the end he took them both and kicked them out of our cabin and along through the iron rails down to the saloon. Fannie was so wild with him, she said they would be all skinned to bits. We got tea and Ernest went at 6 so we went up to the train and saw him off.

After tea we practised, and played all sorts of tunes. The other morning Fannie found a robin's skin under her pillow when she was making her bunk, and she was so wild because she slept on it all night, she called "Moondyne" "Robin" to pay him out for putting it there. We went into the pantry and asked "Robin" for all sorts of things and et pickles and water and anything we could get hold of, we turned in at 10 and slept.

Tuesday
7th October 1890

My birthday, and a lovely fine day. I hate my birthdays I wish I could run away from them all, and O! man, what an old chap I am getting.

We caught the 9 o'clock train and went with Lizzie up to Invercargill. Captain went up with us, when we stopped at the Greenhills station, there was Charlie and "Captain" on the platform they had just ridden over from Greenhills and had stockwhips, and leggins on, they each popped their heads in at the window, Charlie opposite to Fannie and "Captain" by Lillie and yarned away, Lizzie nudged me when she saw Charlie talking to Fannie, and teased her about it after, and we left and saw a man *galloping* after the train, how I longed to be on the horse!! I would have loved a good hard gallop, *as hard as ever* the horse could go – your breath nearly gone and hair streaming back– *oh*! the *joy* of a *real gallop*!

Ernest was at the train station to meet us, coming up in the train Captain was talking to an old beard who bellowed the whole time like a mad buffalo. Ernest went and asked his boss for a holiday, and got it, then we all went strait out to the cemetry we went in and Lillie got some flowers off Ma's mother's grave for her then we came out and waited at the gate while Lizzie went to see a girl I mean a woman called Mrs. Renshaw.

Ernest hammered a small stone into the end of my gamp and went jumping a fence, and scared a youngster by saying "Whats your name? Johnny Dame, who gave you that name? the boys at the village damn 'em". We got tired of waiting for Lizzie so went over to the house she was in and stood by the garden so as she would see us and come out, then we walked halfway back, and Lizzie showed us the house where Lillie and I were born, as we passed and a very humble little shanty it was, something like this to look at painted white and a little paling fence in front. It was funny I should see it today, my birthday for the first time, 20 long years ago I saw it, but being a little muff I didn't take any notice I suppose. We all stood and looked at it for a few minutes, and then went on and got into a tram, O! such a fearful tram that rattled and shook and clacked, and nearly jerked us to atoms. We got out thank goodness, and Lizzie went to some one called Maggie Wells for dinner, and we 3 went with Ernest to his house, and on the way up Pa drove up behind us and took us in a cab to the big water tower place, and up we went and all around, we could see the old Takatimo hills out in front of "Oaklands" from up there, then down and we drove back to Ernest's house for dinner. Ernest would make us go and he went on again with "Stop it Ernest, I wasn't touching yer Ernest" and told Rosa how we went, at dinner he was so mean he was collecting up the plates, and put them all in a pile in front of poor little Charlie and told him to eat up the scraps, and poor little Charlie took up a fork without a word and was going to start eating them when Ernest stopped him, he is the most obedient youngster I ever saw, and Jack is just the opposite, and nearly as showing off as his father. Ernest was so rude he said we would go home and tell Ma (what a horrid dinner he gave us, that leg of mutton was *high* and the pudding *was rotton* –).

They have some lovely pansys so after dinner we got some and Charlie picked mine for me, then all hands and us 3 went to the Cresent to look for Pa and found him walking over the road before we got there, Lizzie saw him. We went and she got something for Ma, and Lizzie would get something for me, and she got me a little ivory cross with a wreath of flowers round it. Back to the train – said goodbye to Rosa and youngsters, Ernest saw us off, we left at 5, and got to the Bluff at 6.

"Captain" and Charlie met us on the platform and came on board with us, and had tea, and after we played, and made them sing, they sang "Killaloo" and Charlie sang ("Bread and cheese and Kisses") "Captain" sang the "Golden Shore" and very nicely too, some of the songs they sang together and they sounded so nice, they sang heaps of others, and we showed them our dressed up photos, and Lillie showed them her photos, then they went. "Captain" had been asking for photos, and Charlie turned round on the stairs from the saloon and said "you wont forget *me*, will you?" we only laughed, but made no rash promises, I shall always see him on the stairs with his legins on and stockwhip in his hand and pinkie cap and one tag of hair in front, and such a pleading voice – then they vanished and we started larking about.

When we came on board, I found a telegram for *me* from Ma saying this "Many happy returns of the day, all well, enjoy trip" – no need to put the last two words to *us* – it's the first telegram I ever got, us 3 and Lizzie sat up and sang songs, and showed off in general, and had "*Whar widna fight for Charlie*? *Whar* and cet" and lots of old roudy songs, to *roudyer* tunes, we shocked Lizzie and she said "did ye iver see sich tirrible children" and "why dont ye sing some of the nice songs Mamma used to sing?" But we were all on for it, regular routed up, and we sang on and laughed, and played, and danced about the saloon, and ate biscuits and drank water, by turns, till "Moondyne" got desperate and turned out the saloon lights, (it was cruel to darken our fairly light hearted spirits in that fashion). Then he chivied Fannie up stairs and round the chart table, and she had to run in our cabin to escape being caught – Captain came suddenly out of his cabin – I think we got tite on water, we had so much, we turned in at 11, and so ended my birthday, a very happy one – yes –

36

Along we go all in a row over the world together.

We get arrested and walked off to the lock-up
on a charge of disturbing the peace of mind
by going over the world together in bags.

Alass!! Alass!!! What shall we do?

We get so thin we squeeze through
the bars & make good our escape.

Our bags fill up with the breeze
and we float off into space

Wednesday
8th October 1890

Woke up to find a most lovely day, after breakfast us three and Lizzie went for a walk to the Ocean beach.

There found a gray – nearly white – mare which we called "Mary" straight off the reel, we made a flax bridle and got on, Fannie and I in turns, then we spotted a riding horse and made a flax bridle for it and saw it didn't mean to be caught, so we crept through the flaxes and got round it.

It gave a start when we hove in view and up with its tail and spurted off between the two of us. We ran at it to give it a whack with the bridle as it got past, then we got a bay mare, called her "Robin" (Lizzie was on the beach picking up shells all this time) We got on and Fannie and I had a ride together, then Lillie and Fannie, then Lillie and me, both our horses were cart horses, and where ever the bay went the white followed it, they had been worked together in harness, the white in the shaft and the bay in the lead. As soon as we got on we called out to Lizzie she looked up and waved her arms and said "O! ye terrible children O! ye terrible children!!" and came up to us, she would make us have her petticote for a saddle-cloth, *white* too of all colours and Lillie gave us hers for the other, but my knickerbockers and stockings were smothered in white hairs off "Mary". Lillie and I rode down to the railway line with our gamps up, to scare the people if the train came past, but it wouldn't come. We mounted our horses on a big gray stone, and under that stone I picked two or 3 little ferns, – I wonder what the owner of the horses would say if they could see us.

Fannie and I rode up to the tangledy bunch of flax and miki miki to get some lovely white suplejack blossom, and got it, we let go our two old cart horses, patted them and made tracks home and Fannie would bring her flax bridle to prove on board we did get a ride, our bitts were nearly chewed thro' altho' we had double flax, Lizzies petticote was almost black with durt off the horses.

Lizzie and Lillie went to a house to get a drink and got a swig of milk, and Fannie and I waited on the road. We came on board, had dinner, and Fannie went to everyone to show her flax bridle, then hung it up in our cabin. We *were* hungry when we got back, it is *such* a lovely day. Oh lovely!!!

38

The "Hinemoa's" ports are under water, she has first a fearful list to port then to starboard from loading coal, we took 200 tons on board, bad stuff too, and were full forrard and aft. After dinner we saw dear Lizzie off by the train at two, poor little old Lizzie when shall we see you again? We were so sorry for her to go, and nearly manned the pumps. Fannie left her shoe to be mended then we came on board again and wrote to Ma and "Montie" (rumors,– a Moffet cometh afar off) – and Lizzie gone, ah gone this lovely day, – we are going to leave at 6, then out on the bounding billows – We went ashore and posted our letters and got Fannies shoe, and tried to get a bottle of fizz, but the owl of a chemist hadn't any, but said he would send us a bottle on board. It *did* come and the old ass that brought it took it below and came on deck and bawled out "I've just taken you down a *bottle* of *medicen*" so everyone could hear, and it was *only Eno's fruit salts after all* – Old Ape! Fannie and I burst out laughing in his face, altho' we were so wild with him, he just wanted all hands on deck to think *we* wanted medicene.

We sat on deck and watched the lovely sunset – we shipped a new 2nd Mate here at the Bluff, and left at 6, and out we go. Captain introduced us to Mr. Moffet, we didn't want him to come, but he came and so did Mr. Pauline who is a fat old buffer, and a fright of a yellow beard called Bar, both scots, and Bar talked like Charlie Duncan. Moffet would stay and yarn to us, till further orders, altho' we were nearly manning the pumps, we were truly sorry to leave the Bluff, and poor little old Lizzie, gone– gone till when? and Lillie said "and us getting older and older till we'll soon be quite ancient and no good at travelling" and so our days go on and on and on.

Lillie said that altho' Pauline and Bar weren't much account they were better than Moffet, Lillie and Fannie still sat on deck till we got round to where we were this morning, lucky time. We all sat looking at the stars, away we go leaving the Bluff and poor old Toi Tois behind *dear* old Toi Tois "yet dost thou recall days departed half forgotten when in dreaming youth I wandered, by the sea–" we didn't turn in till after 9, and soon I slept – and dreampt a funny dream.

39

Thursday

9th October 1890

I dreampt of robbers with guns...

Taking our guns from us, and I thought we were sleeping in our bunks, and Fannie woke me up and said "Merryeanus was looking at her" and I looked, and said "that's not him, but two robbers" and they took the end off my gun, and then there were 3 and one pointed a shot-gun at Lillie, and the other two pointed at Fannie and I, and said if we spoke we would be killed, then I fainted with fright when we were walking away and fell down, and when I came round they were all sitting on the ground waiting for me and I said to the man holding me "surely you would not be such a coward as to kill us?" and he said "yes" then we went on and somehow Fannie and I got away, and we were going to go in the old loose-box at "Oaklands", and get into the loft and hide in the hay, but we found the door fastened, so we got over the door Fannie first, and just as I was getting over, along came "Moondyne" and tryed to stop me, then we were in a big room and people were running about, and then Fannie and I were running away and we both fell down, then King and Harry were there with Ma, and were talking of going up a hill to a bunch of fir trees, and went.

Then I was in my cabin and found on my pillow a handkerchief done up square ways with a tag at one end, I thought it was from "Moondyne', and this was written on the handkerchief in pencil "this is for your birthday as I had nothing at the time". Then I opened it and found folded up grey note-paper in it, I thought it was a letter and was just going to take it out and read it, and I woke up– and all my dreams vanished. It was a strange dream and I cannot write it down half like what it was, it was strange, it was long, and I will not forget it ever.

"Moondyne" woke us and we were at Puysicar Point, (Preservation inlet), anchored and blowing a gale. We got there at 5, and such a lovely morning altho' blowing. We didn't get ashore, as it came on to blow great guns before 8. We got on deck and sang rum songs, and tried to find someone to throw Moffet over board. Fannie asked the mate and "Merryeanus" to do it, but they wernt on, when "Merryeanus" came along we sang *"Whar wouldna fight for Cheeky and etc, boo, boo, boo, boo!!"*. We left at 11 for Dusky sound, blowing half a gale now, we made no headway at all, and had to run to Chalky inlet for shelter, and anchor under or by Chalky Isle and passage Island, we got there before dinner. It is all going black now and such vicious squalls keep coming along hissing over the water as they come.

When we left Puysicar we were watching the waves running up on the rocks all the rocks
were slanting back like big slabs, and the waves ran right up them nearly to the trees,
and all the white foam at the bottom, they were grand to watch. We have "Dorothy" on
board with us, and he stares at us too, and Southerland. We sat on deck and watched the
hands shifting coal aft over the bridge, "Hard at it" (the little brass boy who always looks
empty and half starved) and "Nimble" and the "Oger" which we dont like at all boys,
he's not a bit like a sailor with his plad breeches and shaggy hair and fat self.

It was raining like mad half the time, and "Merryeanus" was showing off a bit, and dabbed
wet coal on Fannies face as he went past. We stayed anchored at the entrance of Chalky Inlet
for the night, after tea the other old chaps played cribbage at the end of the table, Moffet
stayed out of sight for ages, (I wonder did he feel rum? we don't.) then he came down and
sat like a gost at the other end of the table. We said goodnight to "Alabastor" (we called him
that because he looked so gostly and white,) and the others, and went into the pantry to sit
and eat (the pantry was empty). We et a ton of biscuits and drank some water, Lillie choked
me when I was drinking, by making me laugh, and the water came out my nose, we still sat
there, and then went up to bunk. Fannie and I went down again for salt meat, as Lillie had
a bit in her pocket and was eating it in our cabin, we never saw her get it, Fannie got
a handfull of meat while I got the biscuits, we did laugh, and then turn we in.

Friday
10th October 1890

We left Chalky Inlet at four in the morning and got to Dusky Sound at daylight and went up it, we turned out at six and found ourselves going up the sound, it was very wet and waterfalls everywhere.

Then went up "Wet Jacket arm" and landed poor old lonely "Dorothy" by himself and left him there, and I copied his little old shanty, and he had left all his pots and pans and camp ovens out all the time he has been away and his pants hanging on the line. A dear little robin flew on board and settled on the rail and rigging, and hopped about quite tame, the robins were singing everywhere, so nice. We left old "Dorothy" and went on out Breaksea sound, the mist and fog all round was lovely. "Nimble" was wheeling coal over the bridge from forrard and I said "gee up Robin, and wee there steady now" and all sort of things and "Nimble" was grinning at us and upset the coal basket, and up came Captain and saw it and "Nimble" got in for it, and so did "Hard at it" for sitting down and not working. Then he got up on the high up bridge and started cleaning the brass, and I said "there's a steamer out there" and he stopped to look for the steamer but there really wasn't any, then I said "there's a Cape pidgeon". and he looked up at the sky, and he stopped cleaning the brass again to look for the Cape pidgeon. Every time I said anything he stopped and looked, and there was nothing all the time, sometimes he went on cleaning and rubbed all over the white paint while he was looking away, and thought he was doing the brass all the time.

I threw little bits of coal at "Nimble" and Nobery and Martin and the "Oger" when they went along with the coal, they were all grinning and Martin said "thank you". I think he was wild. We were at the top of the companion. Fanny saw an oilskin forrard on the bridge and put it on, and asked what she could do? It was a yellow one belonging to one of the mates, the mate I think, it was miles too big for Fannie, and she asked "Nimble" how much a ride? and he said "a penny". Fannie said "its too much" and asked him if she could not wheel the basket. Arthur gave Fannie a parcel from "Merryeanus" and in it was the scissors, and some black hair off the little cow aft, and some writing to say "the faded flowers were next his heart", and Fannie sent him along some fringed out rope and two verses I made up for her, and here it is.

"That lock of hair I'll always keep
And when you'r dead o'er it I'll weep
And next my heart it there shall stay
Untill I'm clean decayed away.
And 4 the scissors thank I you
And something more I'm bound to do
That is pay you out you see
So hold your whist and bide a wee"

Friday 10th October
1890 EMR.

We got to Milford Sound about 8 or at dark and went up it in the dark and had a bother to find the buoy to make fast to. It bumped and banged against us forrard and it is pitch dark and raining like old boots. We made fast there all night and Captain says its the worst night he's seen in Milford Sd. yet, and the rain is awful, and we turn in early, and slept.

Saturday

11th October 1890

Up at seven and Milford was just lovely, O! the Bowen falls were grand, and I counted sixty waterfalls on the one side of a mountain, and thirty running down the big flat face of rock, there were waterfalls by the hundred, just hundreds.

We landed Southerland and Captain had a barney with him over his passage money, and it *did* rain, and blowing like fury and any waterfall that shot clear of a face or came clear of a ledge, blown up into sprouts of mist. It looked as if dozens of cannons were fired out of the rocks in all directions, truly the dowdyest wretch in the world must have been rejoiced at such a sight. The rain came down in torrents and made such a row on deck.

We left Milford after breakfast and went to Anita Bay at the mouth of the sound, we could not see the tops of the hill for thick mist and fog. We landed stores, and men for Madagascar beach in Anita Bay and there was a cutter anchored under Fox Point, the "Heather Bell". The rain lifted, but it is awfully cold, enough to freeze a brass monkey. The decks were so wet we could not get ashore and Captain told us there was greenstone on the beach, and then we went on to Martin Bay, and too rough to land, too much surf, so we went on to Big Bay and landed Mr Pauline and Bar, they had to come back again for their side of mutton and some lard. We saw the "*red* hills" in the distance and Maori Bills hut on the beach, his real name is Kelly and he ran away from his regiment in the Maori war. He never gets any stores and lives on whatever he can grub out for himself and nothing else.

Lillie was eating oysters (what were in the buckets from the Bluff) all the way back to Martins Bay. I opened some for her and Fannie threw the shells overboard. I tried to make myself eat one but I couldn't, and threw it away. Still too rough to land, so we anchored for the night, it is raining like mad again. Lillie asked Captain if she could have more oysters, he said she could, so she ran up in the rain and took a plate and emptied a bucket and came into our cabin and ate 16, she got rather wet too, as it was pelting. The rain nocked off about tea time, Lillie said she wasn't very hungry at tea, and no wonder. The "Hinemoa" *is* rolling and she dose roll – where will we all be in 80 years? – dead, I suppose – We practised, and wrote, Moffet is quite friendly. We ate about a ton of biscuits and a bottle of water as usual, and turned in happy, Fannie peppered "Moondyne's" cap before she turned in, and we turn in and sleep all night, I sleep with my violin these rough nights I hate it to get banged about and all spoilt.

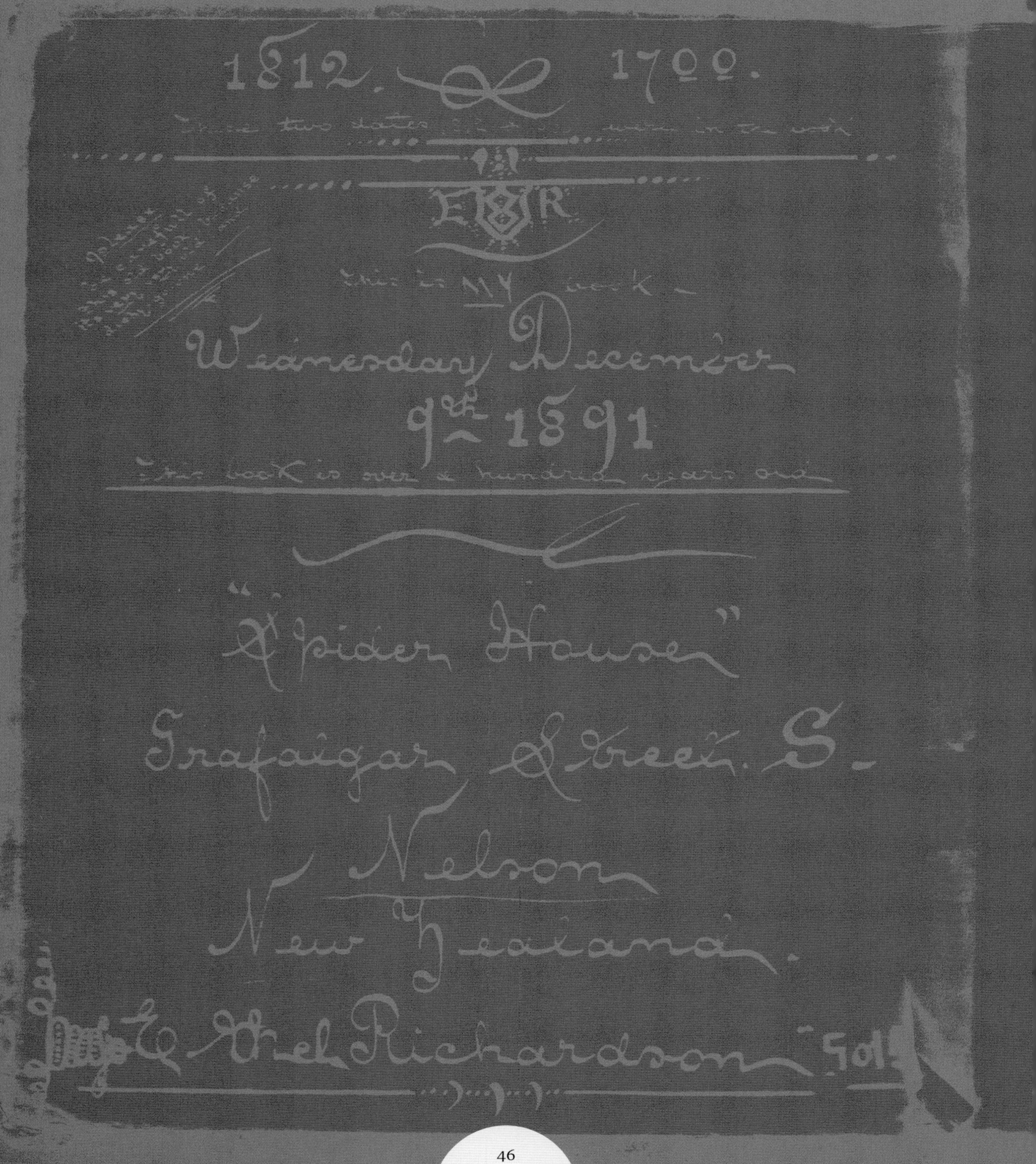

1812. 1700.

these two dates ... written in the book

E R

this is MY work —

Wednesday December
9th 1891

this book is over a hundred years old

"Spider House"

Trafalgar Street. S.

Nelson

New Zealand.

E. Ethel Richardson.

46

DO YOU MEAN TO SAY THESE ARE US?

Sunday
12th October 1890

Up early, still anchored in Martins Bay, Lillie and Fannie had such a wash they flooded out their washing place.

After breakfast we leave for Bruce Bay, it is still too rough to land at Martins Bay, we passed Cascade Point and I copied it out of our port hole.

It was so lovely all waterfalls coming down in streams, we 3 all sat on deck and read all morning. Lillie got a bucket of oysters and et them all, we had to come down as it is raining. We had plum tart for dinner, it was very good and we 3 nearly ate *all* of it. It is blowing too hard so we had to turn in to Jacksons Bay, and got there just after dinner, it is still blowing and raining. We anchored there for the rest of the day and night, Read all afternoon, it *is* cold too. After tea wrote to Ma, and Lillie ate a whole lot more oysters that "Moondyne" and I opened for her, we turned in early, ("Alabastor" turned in first tonight) and knew no more till –

Monday
13th October 1890

Leave Jacksons Bay just twenty minutes after twelve at night, blowing too hard to stop, the wind is blowing in shore and getting worse and we steam off and anchor under "Taumaki Island" for shelter, anchor before breakfast early and stay there, still blowing.

The other name for the island is "Open Bay Island" 13 miles from Jacksons Bay. In the morning we had a practise and fought over it too, we generally end up with a barney. After dinner we 3 Moffet and Captain and 2nd. Mate and Martin and 3 other sailors, went in the boat ashore on the smallest island first to get birds eggs, small seagulls, but found none only one nest, we were too early they were only building. It came on to rain as we were going from the "Hinemoa" to the Island, and we had no ulsters, we put the flags over our knees to keep dry, Captain carried us ashore, and we hated it, Lillie sat on his shoulder, I dont think he found me very light. – The rocks were as sharp as needles, and all jaggy kind and brutal to walk on.

The rocks were as sharp as needles, and all jaggy kind and brutal to walk on.

The boat nearly got stuck putting off, and they had an awful job with the boat as it was rough and shallow, and the tide running out. Then we got in, but wouldn't be carried again altho' Captain wanted us to, we waided out ourselves, but it wasn't deep.

Went to the bigger island, but saw no seals, Captain said there were some there, "Alabastor" shot 3 shags with one shot, one on a nest, got two of them, and left the 3rd as we couldn't get it, they were a very rare kind and only found there on the island. We were wild with Moffet for shooting the poor beautiful birds. We saw scroms of shags all sitting on their nests there were just hundreds, Captain jumped ashore and got some eggs, 5 in his hat, the shags all have crests. Then we pull back to the "Hinemoa" and came on board wet as it had been raining heavy, it was pretty rough. "Gilpin" cleaned the eggs for us, they all had chickens in them. We went aft and had a look at the little black heiffer, she is awfully thin, and started to eat Moffet's overcoat.

Lillie had a big wash today 5 handkerchiefs and a pair of stockings, we are always washing stockings and snuffpokes, and hanging them up to dry in our cabin on the brass rail in front of the port. Lillie and Fannie were playing at the two bobbies trying to out do one another on duty round the chart table and main mast. Lillie was "Thompson" and Fannie "Beattie", I was in the saloon and heard them, they made such a row running round and laughing,

I was laughing down below too. Lilllie got a bucket of oysters and ate them and Fannie went for the corkscrew and we opened the cocoanut, when we got all the milk out we each had our whack then wrinced it out with water and drank it but it wasnt very nice though. Then Fannie got a tommy-hawk from Arthur and broke the cocoanut, we gave some to Captain and Arthur then ate the rest.

Then we had hide-and-seek. Lillie and Fannie hid from me, and after tea we had it again, and we hid in the bathroom out side and in the engine room. We were laughing at "Alabastor" trying to whistle "Our Jack" but he was very good and didn't tell of us hiding. Fannie and I hid in "Moondyne's" cabin and Fannie laid on Arthur's bun and flattened it out hiding on his bunk. Arthur wouldn't tell Lillie where we were, but grinned the whole time and seemed to enjoy the joke, he wouldn't have been so joyfull if he knew his hat was squashed flat, I hid in the pantry behind the door and Arthur scrubbed the floor so Lillie shouldn't know I was there, and when Fannie was hiding in "Moondyne's" cabin she had "Moondyne's" white pants over her head and never knew it. We laughed and romped away till we were roasted. I practised exercises on my violin the whole afternoon nearly. In the evening I played draughts with Fannie then Moffet. "Nimble" is the watchman and it is pouring cats and dogs, and blowing great guns too, and the waves keep thumping like thunderbolts against the "Hinemoa's" sides. We are anchored here for the night now, we turned in at 10. I had to go down again for my fiddle case, I left it on the saloon table, and all the lights were out, and I saw Arthur fumbling about in his bunk with his head out, the cabin door was open. I picked up my violin and ran, and "Moondyne" said "drop it" I said "I wont!" and flew up stairs and into our cabin, we were soon asleep – and into the far off Land of Dreams–*–

Tuesday
14th October 1890

Leave Open Bay Island at three a.m. and make for Bruce Bay. We woke up early and found ourselves going to Bruce Bay, it was very rough and wet, and we got there at breakfast time, and too rough to land, too much surf on, we anchor and stay rolling about like a stricken antelope.

In the morning before dinner we were in the pantry, and "Gilpin" caught us at the tins of biscuits, eating, the three of us, he didn't say anything but glared at us. We saw a bottle of nice preserved plums *we thought*, and asked "Moondyne" if we could have some?, he said "yes" and opened the bottle for us and had some himself. We each tasted them– *O! lor*!! they were *olives* – we spit them out into the rubbish bucket in the corner pretty quick too, they tasted of oil and O! lor! no more Spanish olives for us – then Fannie asked if there was any lime juice on board? "Moondyne" said "no" but gave us a tin of apricots (good old customer) and opened them for us too. We got a plate and 3 spoons and went up to our cabin to eat them. We put as much out of the tin as would get on the plate and started *even* having a *spoonfull turn about*, a bite, and juice, we kept on ("now a bite and now juice") we laughed

52

over the eating business till we were limp. Fannie and I fought over the juice that was left in the plate, and while we were arguing Lillie ate out of the tin and was getting a double dose. Lillie said Fannie was jealous, Fannie said "no, only greedy". We threw the tin out the port hole when we had done, and washed our plate and spoons, and put them back. We did have a feast.

We had dinner and still too rough to land, just before dark the boat went ashore and landed, awfully rough. Letters went ashore so we posted two to Ma it came on a SowWest gale, Captain blew the whistle for the boat to hurry back. Before the boat got long side it was blowing great guns, we went off for Jacksons Bay as hard as we could peg, as soon as the boat was hoisted inboard, with furious head wind and got there at a quarter to 11 and anchored on the *wrong side* of the point in the rough water, and she *did* roll. I had my violin in bunk to help chock me off and save it at the same time. Lillie felt *rum* and turned in at 8, we did not get much sleep for the everlasting rolling.

Wednesday
15th October 1890

At daylight we went round and anchored in Jacksons Bay in shelter, and stay there all day, we rolled about awfully in the night and were nearly "smashed to atoms" it was fine, calm, and cold but came on to rain and blow again before breakfast.

We were having fun on the deck Lillie and I were two horses "Charlie" and "Harry" and Fannie was driver with her old yellow scarf for reins, driving us up and down the deck, and after breakfast us 3 and Moffet went ashore in Robinsons boat and "Merryeanus" too and then directly we got ashore we went up the hill and into the top track for ferns, and we went to past the creek in the bush, and O! the ferns!!! the ferns, the ferns! they were so lovely, no body can tell what they are like, you must see to know and have eyes that *can* see too, the kidney ferns were in millions, up the stem of every tree almost and plastered all over the ground in *beds and beds, and beds,* and the polly poddies miles long and hanging down in O! such bunches, and umberalla ferns *O!!* – that's all I can say. We hopped around with delight, pure joy at such a lovely place, who wouldn't hop? We *yelled*, and *danced*, and *sang* bits of songs at every pretty place we came to till we were so limp we could *only point.*

We ran down the track every here and there and said ("*hay!! hay!! hay!!*") the ferns were *so* lovely we didn't know what to do, we wished all our friends could only see it. We went a good way past the creek, and every time we ran down a steep place we hoisted up our dresses and ran in our knickerbockers so as we could take proper big strides, and we *did* take strides, we went so quick down the hollows that we went half way up the other side before we could stop. We found a funny kind of fern something like a "hounds tongue" only it grows very big and very wee, we kept on "Lillie!!" "Fannie!!" "Ethel!! the whole time to make each other look, and "*can't you look*? – *can't you look at mine then – will* you look?" "O! *look what your missing*! – can't you just look at what I'm showing you?"

55

Running down the track at Jacksons Bay

Fannie gets bogged in moss and calls to Lillie for help

We saw the same ferns Lillie and Nina looked at last time, Lillie was getting some umberalla ferns and Fannie yelled out "quick, quick, I bogged" and so she was too, bogged up to her knees in moss and mud, and old logs nearly up to her waist, and I called out "wait a minute till I come and see you". We fairly roared laughing at her, and Lillie could hardly pull her out for laughing, the moss was most beautiful in *piles* and *piles* and *piles* just heaps of green moss and all wet and such lovely earth for flowers. All the time the birds were singing, no wonder we were happy, no wonder.

We ran with young legs and light hearts, the robins were singing everywhere their dear little clear voices ringing out in the silent gullies one close and when it stops one further off still going and the old Tuis, "chow chow chuckle chuckle chow chow chow," and sucking in sound they make and mocking birds and all kinds. – We were coming along in fine style in knickerbockers and dresses hauled up, talking at the rate of knots and there was "Merryeanus" and Robinson, we nearly ran slap into them but our dresses were down before they saw us. They were after cattle and asked us had we seen them? We said yes, we saw them back a bit, we went back and showed them where they were and helped hunt them up and drive them back. One was to be killed for fresh meat. Coming back we got behind and got ferns, and we got thistles for the cow and gotes and sheep, then we caught up to "Merryeanus" out by the open. He was cutting ruby sticks to wollop the sea lions he said. "Merryeanus" made us wait so he would not miss his dinner, he had an awful wee tommy to chop with. We said "we're going down to the boat to go off to dinner" and he said "O that would be mean," as the boat would go off if we went down and did not wait for him if he was the only one left. He told us to wait for him as he was hungry and wanted his dinner, so we waited, but every now and then we said "we're off" and made out we were going. He said "O! mercy ye wouldn't be so mean". Lillie was picking some beautiful big bramble blossom and it came off with a jerk and she sat clean down backwards on the track and "Merryeanus" had to pull her up again, we did laugh.

We went down to the boat and I was talking to an old grey beard who introduced himself as Mr. Stevens and he said he married a Miss Loyd, and said he knew Pa and all of us and was at "Oaklands" and asked did unkle Malley once live in Fiji and did he marry a widdow! and about a thousand and one questions about Aunt Fanny. I let Lillie answer him and she answered as if she knew all about it (?) "Merryeanus" picked two big drum lilly blossoms and brought on board, there were some growing buy the edge. We just caught the boat nicely and went off without "Alabastor" as he did not turn up he was away shooting.

Had plum tart at dinner we 3 had it, and ate nearly all of it. What ever one has we all have the steward says "what will you take Miss Lillie?" – "tart please" – "Miss Ethel?" – "tart please" – "Miss Fannie?" – "tart please" and then we all laugh. Fannie and I fed the goats and sheep, and cow, with thistles and Lillie pressed ferns. The poor cow is nearly starved they have no food on board for her. We went ashore again. "Alabastor" got no dinner, and he went along the bottom track. "Gilpin" came too, and the 2nd. Mate was squatting down eating cress and putting some in one of the buckets and I went up to him and asked what time the boat was going off again? We thought he was an awful ape because he only stared at me and never answered at all, so off we went along the bottom track this time and every patch of good thistles we came to we cut them and left them in a pile to get on the way back, some of them such beauties and as high as us, such a feast for the poor little cow. On the way out we met "Alabastor" returning just by the steep face of rock. We stopped and got some lovely big kind of creeping everlasting daisys they grew along the top of the rock and Lillie climbed half way up and got some and I went round and got on top and threw them down to Fannie.

Two road men passed us there, half way along old Stevens caught us up and walked past the school and yarned about all the old frumps in the days of Adam. I patted a cow that was on the track and he said "just look at that dreadfull sister of yours, I wouldn't care to do that they might give you a kick or a poke" and he said "Captain Fairchild is a very gruff old man" and Lillie said "*I like him*" and old Stevens said "yes, oh yes, he is a very nice man, a very nice man" sly old animal. He left us by the school, and we passed a little fenced in place with graves in it, then turned out to the beach to see the Arawata river, but it was a good way off so turned we back and came back to our track, and we had a jump over a creek crossing the track. We galloped at it and jumped it two or three times, it was a dear little creek all grass to the very edge just past it in the ditch and swampy place we saw some lovely ferns.

Bringing back thistles for the cow & sheep, Jacksons Bay.

We said good bye to old Stevens, and passed a man and a woman and a pack horse going to the settlement – the horse was brown and only had one eye. We got some musk it was growing every where and by all the creeks, and the sent of it was *just Heavenly*, I *love* it. We collected up our thistles and got lots of Koromiko too for the cow, I got so many thistles I could hardly walk home.

We got to the beach just as the boat came off, and waited for a bit, "Merryeanus" and no end of ferns (sensitive) came off in our boat, and "Hard-at-it' too and he was all soaking wet from carrying moss. "Alabastor" came off in Robinsons boat with the beef, the 2nd. Mate threw stones in the water for us to step on to get to the boat. There were such a lot of lovely creeks in the bush this morning we got a drink at one, and the old snowy mountains in the distance looked lovely showing thro' a gap in the track, and the "Hinemoa" close in, in the smoothe water, and far out the sea all white breakers its so rough. We saw a kaka and 2 pidgeons today, we saw a lovely rainbow this evening and went on board for tea. Had tea and gave the cow a feed of thistles and koromiko and the sheep and goats too and after tea we pressed ferns, and my hand would not stop shaking after carrying the thistles more than 2 miles.

Lillie and Fannie went and got a drink out of the can that was hanging up in the outside bathroom, (we got fresh milk here) we thought the steward might give us some, so we kept on saying *"we are so thirsty"* , "and we cant drink the water its horrid" and directly "Moondyne" came in the saloon we started louder than ever – "we're so thirsty!" so he sat the water bottle on the table in front of us and 3 glasses, so we couldn't say anything. So Fannie and I went up and out to get some milk for ourselves, and Lillie went in our cabin and talked quite loud to make out we were all there, but it was too dark and we daren't strike a light or we might have been caught,– we turned in early and slept sound – and knew no more till light again.

Thursday
16th October 1890

*"I am day; and bring again
Life and glory, love and pain;
- Awake, arise!" -*

At 1 am, early we left Jacksons bay, and went to Cascade Pt. and so rough we had to turn back, and got back to Jacksons bay, and anchored. It's lovely and calm in here, but awful rough outside, we could not go to Martins Bay, we put our boots on deck to dry and brushed our dresses, and after breakfast went ashore with "Alabastor". We made him ask for horses for us, we were dying for a ride, but worse luck they were all gone to Smooth Water Bay, so we went with "Alabastor" along the bottom track to the steep face of rock. We were looking for pidgeons for Moffet to shoot, I spied one sitting on a branch away up on a high tree. "Alabastor" shot it and went to look for it and he could not find it *great muff* – and came out as wild as he could stick, all clawed to bits and his boots full of rubbish. He sat down and took them off and said he thought the ferrets had collared the pidgeon as he saw some feathers and couldn't find it so Fannie and I said we'd go and get it. He said we couldn't find it and we said *we could,* and went, while Lillie got some daisys off the rock and Moffet went for more pidgeons.

Fannie and I had a job to get to the tree, which was the first thing. I got right under the branch the pidgeon was on then looked to lu'ard the way the breeze would carry the feathers and soon found the feathers – one or two – a few yards from the tree and then went back a bit straight for the tree where I knew I *must* find the pidgeon, but all this was easier said than done, it was on the side of a gulley and all old fallen trees crawling in Kei Kei and undergrowth, and lawyers and big beautiful ferns. Fannie and I kept saying "have you got it?", "no, have you?", "no", "we must get it, keep on looking" – at last I found a patch of feathers where it had fallen, and I looked and looked, and at last I found it away under a big old tree stem, it had rolled away under and the thick ferns kept me from seeing it. "I've got it" said I and we got out pidgeon and all and we came back glad and gave Moffet his game. No wonder *he* could not find it being in a town all his days, we were used to finding ducks and pidgeons for Pa when we used to go shooting with him at "Oaklands".

61

A man came past on a nice little black horse and Fannie asked if she could have a ride, but he was a surley customer and would hardly answer, soon Mr. Mackfarlin and a boy came on a nice little black something like "Brisk" called "Maori" and a raw boned old bay called "Buss", Fannie asked for a ride and Mr. Mackfarlin let Fannie ride his black but lead it as it was young and half wild, it was a pretty little colt and had such nice legs. Mr. Mackfarlin had a kitten in a bag and Lillie carried it back for him and carried it more comfortable than he would too. "Alabastor" got two more pidgeons on our home ward journey. We were going to get "Buss" for a ride after dinner *hurrah*! *boys*!!! We missed the last boat, and had to wait on the beach for the dingy, we had more food for the cow and sheep and "Hard-at-it" and Arthur came off for us, they pulled *fine not a bit crooked* about as straight as *a rams horn*. We went on board and we had a gooseberry tart for dinner it was very good and we were *very hungry*, as usual we all went for it, and after dinner Lillie got a tin and planted the daisy roots, then we went ashore again, with Arthur and "Hard-at-it" for crew. I took the stroke oar as they were enough to make you ill to see them pulling.

Fannie riding old Buss at Jacksons Bay

Mr Mackfarlin gave us old "Buss" to ride and a man's saddle too, and Fannie got on and went past the school away out to the flat. Lillie and I walked on and got stuff for the cow then sat down and ate some of Miss Sinclair's cake, we still had some left, and took it with us to eat and some biscuits. We sat on the road till Fannie came back. A boy came past and a man on a bay cart horse called "Billie" Lillie said to the boy "have you seen my sister" he said "yes, I saw Miss Richardson riding" I wonder how he knew the name? – I washed my snuffpoke at one of the creeks and tied it on to a pronged stick to dry – so fashion

and carried it along like a banner over my shoulder till it got dry. Lillie had a ride next and Fannie and I walked on and stopped at a lovely little creek all grass to the edge and a fern tree growing almost in it and got a drink and soaked our biscuits in it and ate them – they were grand too. Then I had a ride and "Buss" wanted to come home, I had a canter along the sand on the beach, and came back full tilt and there were "Alabastor" and Mr. Mackfarlin, and "Alabastor" looked rather shocked to see *me* on straddle legs, *I didn't care*, I spose he saw a bit of knickerbockers. He had been shag shooting and didn't get any. We said goodbye to Mr. Mackfarlin.

Arthur "Hard-at-it" and Gilpin took us off, when we were coming ashore after dinner little Charlie was in a terrible funk and said we would be on the rocks in a few minutes, because he saw the stones ahead where we were landing. After tea it was rather cold and we went on deck, it is a lovely evening and a young moon setting down behind the bush, Lillie and Fannie walked up and down the bridge and I stood leaning over the rail and thinking – and watched the shadows, made by the faint moonlight going slowly backward and forwards across the deck with the motion of the vessel.

63

cascade point   12th 10. Sunday 90

We could see the snowy old mountains too, the sea is getting quite calm, (before it was dark Fannie and "Alabastor" played stag-knife on the bridge). We went below and I practised, then we practised together, Fannie shut "Moondyne" in the bathroom, she kept on teasing him in the saloon, so he grabbed her up to put in her spare bunk out of the way, Fannie said *"I'll make you let go*!" and grabbed his moustache – cruel little beggar – The sea has gone down a good bit, and we went and sat in the pantry and ate biscuits, and we got awfully thirsty and Fannie asked "Moondyne" what he kept in the jugs hanging up? as a hint for milk, he said "all sorts of things" so Fannie asked straight out for some, and he gave us a jug full to take up. He was a *brick*, the milk was *lovely* Lillie and Fannie enjoyed theirs to the last degree, but I put some Eno's Fizz into my last glass to see how it would go, and up it came! talk of froth!! it fizzed up and up and *filled two glasses and ran over* then it went all beastly and turned into *pure froth* I said "what ever is up with it?" Lillie and Fannie did laugh loud we all laughed till we were limp over it and Fannie *fairly roared* my word we did laugh. And we turned in and the doors kept on *click* – clack,– *click* – clack, all together, those that were clached open, with the gentle roll.

Friday
17th October 1890

Three weeks since we left Wellington, and we left Jacksons Bay at eleven last night, and got to Martins Bay at daylight around five and they landed (but not us) and off again at six, for Thompson Sound, but very cold and fine all day.

Fannie and Lillie went on deck before breakfast, the snowie mountains were lovely and clear, we 3 walked up and down the deck for a long time this morning, and we got into Thompson Sd. just after 12, and the sea is very calm and came out Doubtfull Sound. We went round Secretary Island, two poor dogs were left on it once, and coming out of Doubtful Sound we had fine fun we told Moffet we could go up one of the steepest places in *10 minutes* (really too steep to get up *at all*), and he said we *couldn't* and we said *we could*.

Fannie rubbed some seed off the creeping daisy on Lillie and I and all over Lillie's ulster. We were at the top of the companion sitting, and Lillie threw the daisies overboard, so Fannie grabbed off Lillie's cap, so she ran down for Fannie's old yellow scarf and made out to wipe her nose on it, so Fannie took her garment, and Lillie took hers, then they put away garments, and came up again, and went for caps. Fannie grabbed Lillie's cap and Lillie grabbed hers, and hung on, and Fannie said "let go" and Lillie said "let go" and Fannie said "let go" and Lillie said "let go" and they kept it up for a long time, hanging on to each others heads, and Martin was laughing at them and the 2nd. Mate, I was curled up with laughing, no wonder they laughed – I gave Fannie a ride on the little coal trolley affair up and down the bridge, and nearly ran her off at the end.

"Alabastor" went to sleep on the seat lying down, we told him to tell us what he dreampt of, he said he would, but never did. We hid down below, and played *lovely* tunes on the piano, and banged "Moondyne" with cushions, and went and ate all the watercress out of the bucket that the 2nd. Mate got, and biscuits by the ton in the empty cabin opposite the pantry. Then we went in the pantry and yarned to "Moondyne" and "Gilpin" came in and I promised him a bottle of vinegar on his wedding day. When Fannie and I came out by the Fidley hiding the men started shovelling down coal and Fannie and I had to scramble up on the bridge out of the way, there wasn't any ladder either.

It was so pretty in the sound, and lots of cow fish swimming round, and any amount of snow, and my word it was cold, there were heaps of lovely fern trees out by the opening of the sound. At half past 5 we passed the "Five Fingers" named by Capt. Cook, about 6 we had a fine view of the entrance of Dusky Sound and the snowie mountains far up it looked lovely, it is clouding up for a Sou-west gale and the glass has fallen more, and still falls. As we came out of the Sound we saw a whole lot of penguins diving.

We put into Puysicar Point to send letters ashore about 10, it was dark Lillie and Fannie wrote to Ma, and nearly all afternoon us 3 sat in the pantry and yarned with "Moondyne" and "Gilpin", he is about 34 and "Moondyne" 28 last birthday. After tea us 3 sat in the saloon and "Moondyne" showed us how to play "Kiscener" and two tricks with the cards, and squeezing water out of a match, we waited up to see the light, it was just like a search light and very pretty. Captain took the letters ashore and our one to Ma, it was very dark and lightening and thunder, and the glass still falling at the rate of knots. We ate our biscuits in the pantry I sat on the shelf, Fannie kept on teasing "Moondyne" so he carried her up to bunk, Fannie said *"isn't he a darned old–"* then *thump thump thump on his head with her pen*–!! Lillie and I laughed till we were limp, then we turned in at 11– and made tracks for the Snares – and here endeth one more day –

Saturday
18th October 1890

Ladies and Gentlemen this is my book please–

Wake up and find ourselves anchored in Mason Bay, Stewart Isd, up early, and cold and cloudy.

After breakfast go ashore and "Hard-at-it" and Arthur pull us ashore, and us three and "Alabastor" and Captain go up the side of the Island after sheep (It was one of the Ernest Islands we were on) (there are two of them,) and we went over most of the Island and it was awful hard to get along the scrub was so thick, we saw three new kind of scrub, all pretty and we got torn to pieces.

"Alabastor" shot two sheep for fresh meat but they were so thin Captain said they were no good it was an awful waste to shoot them and leave them, they were so starving they were eating the flax leaves right down to the roots. One poor sheep had a bit of flax in its mouth when Moffet shot it. Captain started to try and catch an old ewe lamb, so we joined in the chase and we ran down the sheep and lamb, they ran in the bush when Captain ran after them, and he went in after them and they came out on the sand then we caught the sheep and Fannie caught the lamb, it was so done with running it just fell in some cutting grass and just lay there. We were *so sorry* we ran after it then, and the poor old mother was so done too she fell down.

Captain said they were no good and to let them go, they were *so* thin, the mother got up again and ran away, then we followed her tracks to try and let the lamb go so it could see her, but the old sheep kept on going off, and Captain called to us to come to the boat, so Fannie and I went down to let him know Lillie was letting the lamb go where it could find its mother. We were so sorry for the poor little lamb, it was so thin and tired and just lay still against Lillie when she was sitting down, and kept on looking up at us, poor little beggar its down right cruel to leave the sheep on the Island. Lillie carried the lamb through some scrub, and got into it and found it was too thick to go on, and so had to come out again, and it was jolly hard to do that. Lillies hat got nocked off, and her hair all clawed down and her dress torn to atoms, and she was *scratched* and *clawed* in all directions, she let the poor little lamb go just about where we caught it. It went slowly up the sand poor little beggar it was just about done for, I think it will soon find its mother when she starts baaring for it I hope it finds her all right. All this time Captain kept on coo-ee-ing for Lillie and said she must be lost and Fannie and I were so wild because we knew she was all right. Coming off it came on to rain hard and blow too, Fannie and I pulled and let Arthur and "Hard-at-it" have one oar between them, they made such a mess of pulling, we couldn't pull properly. Their oar was up to heaven when our two were in the water, and when ours were out theirs was a mile under, Captain kept telling us to pull or we'd never get off and they were in such a fluster they kept thumping us in the back with the oar, Fannie and I were so wild with them – we got on board we just got off in time as it came on to some purpose and *blew* – hissing the water up in front of the squalls –and here we are anchored and the wind blowing. At dinner "Alabastor" ate a tart and changed plates with Captain after he had gone up, so the steward would think he had eaten it. Fannie hid 3 tarts, one for each under the dish cover to eat after and "Alabastor" did too when he saw us. Lillie and I mended our dresses after dinner and Fannie practised then I copied some music *"Off she goes"*.

After tea practised and hid, Lillie and I hid one time and Lillie had on "Alabastors" cap and overcoat and I had on "Moondyne's" cap and overcoat and we went and stood out by the engine room, so when Fannie came and looked, in the half dark she would think we were two men and not think it was us at all and –***, and a sudden fluff of wind came down from over the top of the fidley *and blew "Moondyne's" cap overboard* – I said *"Lillie!!!"* and grabbed her by the arm, we ran to the side and watched it settle gently under the lee of the ship – in to the dark water, I said "Lillie how on earth can we get it?" and we followed it along, *the wretch*!!!! – lord, I was in a funk, we didn't know what to do, Fannie appeared on the scenes and we told her all about it and I know she would never have known us. I went in overcoat and all *and hatless too* and looked down over the rail into the saloon and called out "Moondyne", – your cap has gone overboard!!" he only said "is it!" and didn't seem to believe me at first, but I told him again and said *"it really has"*. I was hardly game to show up – We stopped hiding then, and went below and "Moondyne" showed us the match trick, and one with a penny, and we gave riddles, and we made them play *"rabbit"*, and quakers wedding, we went in the pantry and got some biscuits, and "Moondyne" told us his cap was a new one and cost 3 half crowns – thats 7/6, it was silk I know so I told him I would buy him a new one when we got back to Wellington, he started to get wild and said I'd do nothing of the kind. We yarned till a quarter to 12, and turn in.

69

Pie of our pidgeons from Jacksons Bay

Sunday
19th October 1890

Still anchored in Mason Bay, and fine but very cold and just blowing great guns from the Sou West, and after breakfast us three walk up and down, and it is blowing just as hard and cold cold cold! –

We three ran up and down the deck to get warm, and the dingy went ashore without us, – mean beggars – and "Alabastor" too and never asked us, they went to the other island too, "Alabastor" went and took his gun, and "Merryeanus" in the bows, and Miller the second engineer, and both Mates, and Noberry and "Nimble", and two or three sailors, we never new they were off till they came pulling along past us.

We ran to the side and asked why didn't they take us? – the Mate said "do you wish to come" and I said "don't answer, let him yelp for nothing" and we didn't, but only looked at them with disappointed faces and just as they got round the bows, spray went all over the boat and "Merryeanuses" cap blew off and we called out *"serve you right, serve you right"* and laughed at them. Fannie and I ran up to the foc'sle, and looked at them, watched them go ashore, and longed to go too.

We fed the old black goat with the 3 little ones, with potato's, there wasn't a soul forrard, or anywhere about, then we all sat up by the bread locker. We had our ulsters on, and old scalves, and I told a yarn of a "Geni" living in a scrub, and Lillie told a yarn of the two middies called "Bill" and "Robin", and the girl called "Lilac", then we sang poetry about them all going ashore and leaving us, to the tune of *"You are rude Madam"* I went down for a pencil and bit of paper to make a bit of poetry about them and did. We all helped to make it up and had grand fun over it, and I just showed it to Moffet too, when they came on board. It's jolly mean to be a girl, the men hate you going with them – we hated ourselves and wished we wern't – we could see they didn't want us, they got away so quiet – girls are more plague than profit, usless *little brutes*, I spose they thought we'd be such a bother, would we then? and now for our lovely poetry, we thought it was *grand*.

S. S. "Hinemoa" Oct 19th. 1890
Sunday Mason Bay Stewarts Island E. R.

Three girls went for a morning walk,
and first thing they did find
A white horse nodding over a fence
and him they left behind.
One said "its a white horse"
the others they said "nay!"
Its but a Government Officer
in a nightshirt for the day.

————————

("look here") -
I wish it was this old day again.

"Milk-and-water" and "Moondyne" potted at seagulls aft, and Fannie went for them and scolded them, one of them threw a potato at Fannie, so she got some too and threw at them. The others came back before dinner, and Fannie scolded them all in turns for not taking us. "Merryeanus" caught Fannie by our cabin and gave her a bristle scrubbing, *cheeky old beggar!!* Then we went and sat by the fidly in the sun, where it was warm and out of the wind, and Fannie shied potatoes at the men as they took away their dinner, and one fireman offered her a jam tart, but she didn't take it. "Gilpin" came out and gave us a bit of greenstone which we all wanted. We had pidgeon pie for dinner with the feet out of the top of the crust, and we had apricot tart it was very good.

After dinner "Moondyne" put 5 tarts in our cabin, he was a brick, we then ate them, by degrees he got crabid, and it rained like old boots in the afternoon and Lillie wrote to Lizzie, two sheets of foolscap, After tea we sat round the fire and "Alabastor" too, and told ghost storys till ten, "Moondyne" went into his cabin, (as a hint for us to go too I spose,) and we all turned in, still at Mason Bay and blowing still. Yesterday Fannie and I wanted to get the dingy and go ashore for the two sheep Moffet shot, we said they'd do for stews or something, we could have easy hauled them down to the dingy and taken them off if Captain had let us, but he wouldn't, but we did want to get them all the same.

Monday
20th October 1890

We left Mason Bay at two in the morning for the Snares, and it was too rough so we put into Wilson Bay and anchored just before breakfast, and here we are and it is cold and blowing like old boots.

Lillie woke up with a sudden start, as she got a fine dose of salt water in her port and all down her neck and in her ear, and all over her bunk, her port was open and so was Fannie's she got a fine dose too. Lillie got up and fixed up her bunk, and the things on the table, we were rolling most awfully and Lillie woke Fannie as the water was all streaming down onto her bunk on top of her. It is fine but very cold, after breakfast Lillie and Fannie ran round the sky-light on the deck trying to catch one another, Fannie had a flax leaf and gave Lillie fits with it when she didn't get out of her way quick enough. As usual "Hard-at-it" stopped work to watch the fun, and Lillie said "O! look at that big beast!" and he looked to where they did, but don't suppose he saw the beast – as there was none to see–!! Fannie got some paint from "Nimble" to put on "Merryeanus" but he didn't come. – This morning Fannie found one of the pidgeons feet in her bunk

Pigeon foot

72

she had slept on it all night and didn't know, so she brought it down and put it in "Moondyne's" bunk. He and "Merryeanus" were fixing up the dead lights in the saloon, and Fannie was teasing them and she put some paint on "Merryeanus" and he gave her a scrubbing.

Fannie told him that "he thought of nothing but kissing from morning to night" and he said "well any pretty girl is worth kissing" and Fannie said "it's a wonder you don't put a skirt on a pair of tongues and *kiss it.*" and he said "I wouldn't mind if the skirt belonged to a nice girl" and Fannie said "*old daddy Knox,* you haven't given up spooning yet" and he said "*O its rather good fun sometimes.*" and he took Fannies precious wooly cap and put it on, and she went and banged "Moondyne" with a cushion for not helping her get back her cap, so he shut her in his cabin, and left her there, so she tied up everything she could get hold of into knots, to teach him not to shut her up in a hurry again.

We practised before dinner, and after it Lillie mended, and Fannie and I practised it was very wet and cold in the afternoon the boat went ashore for water, and to get some food for the cow. Moffet went with them, and brought Lillie back some ferns and moss. "*D*** 'im*" Lillie said, she didn't want to sort them all up and press them they were such a bother, and some rum flat plant with big leaves like rubarb, they saw a big Sydney cedar log on the beach, it was 18 feet long, and just before tea about 5 we went from Wilson Bay round to port Pegasus and got there in good time before dark, and after tea the dingy went ashore and they wouldn't let us go.

The ones that went in the boat ashore were "Gilpin" "Alabastor" "Merryeanus" the "Lizzard" and the two Mates, they saw an old man living by himself at the store, we wanted some things at the store but the old man had hardly enough for himself. "Alabastor" had on 3 coats when he went ashore, to keep warm, he got some tin specimens and brought back, it is fine and calm in here, and one house ashore and no more, but it was cold, *awfully cold.* Lillie and Fannie walked up and down the deck after tea, then Lillie pressed ferns and moss, and Fannie and I put stuff in "Nimbles" boots and tied them to the iron bars in the fidley and I have no more to write just now, so will shut up for a little while – * * * Fannie and I played grab, and we squatted round the fire and I went to sleep – then I got some biscuits and we roasted them, and ate them. We soaked some in a glass of water and roasted them for a change and then roasted some and then soaked them, they were grand. It is fine and calm this evening, but it *was* blowing this afternoon, *hard,* and frantically cold into the bargin, and wet, and we turned in about eleven. When I finished washing and turned in it was 12, and the anchor was just going up, and we started for the Snares once more, and just got out and it was too rough, so we had to turn back and anchored lower down and slept we, and we slept, till day again.

Tuesday

21st October 1890

Here we are anchored lower down in Port Pegasus, and we saw four big king penguins swimming close to the port hole in the saloon, it is very cold, and it kept on raining and hail squalls, hard, the deck was white, it is blowing a regular Sou West gale, and the glass has gone down to twenty-eight, eighty-two, lower than it has been since eighteen sixty.

One of the hands got a cut on the head, a bit of coal fell on him down in the hold. It did blow cats and dogs. After dinner I made draught men 14 of each "Moondyne" got me the wood and helped to cut them out at least he cut *one*, and "Alabastor" one, and Fannie cut out 7, and I did the rest 19 of them, I cut my thumb too. Lillie pressed moss, and practised, and then waisted the rest of the day sitting round the fire. We went aft and saw the Sea hawk. After tea I fadilised the draught men by carving on them, and made the other two, Arthur got me two chissels from the carpenter to make them with, "Alabastor" wrote out verses of latin for Fannie. We couldn't go on deck it was blowing too hard, and it was a wild night – we are anchored by the South arm, and it is very pretty in the harbour, we turned in at 11, and had soon forgotten all –

Wednesday
22nd October 1890

Still anchored down by the mouth of Port Pegasus, and a fine morning, but cold and still blowing hard outside, and the glass falling again, and two boats have gone ashore, and left us again.

The dingy went and got food for the cow and sheep, then went out fishing and stayed out till after dinner. Captain was so wild with them for staying away so long with Charlie in the boat. He said he would be starved with the cold and half dead, poor little beggar, no wonder, he had hardly any cloths on, and sitting still in the boat he must have been fairly frozen. They didn't get many fish. I dreampt so plain of Fred and the two Clares this morning, I can't write down all.

Lillie and Fannie danced on deck while I blackened all my draught men in the saloon. I got the ink bottle, and stuck a pen nib into the men and then dipped them in the ink and held them there for a minute to let the ink soak in, and they looked fine when they came out, and I put them on the ink stand in a row to dry.

The big boat went for water and just got back in nice time for dinner, they saw two seals and a crane up the harbour, Lillie and Fannie and "Alabastor" fed the cow with potato pealings, she was *so hungry* and fought the sheep for the pealings. We sat on the hatch by the sea-lions cage in the sun, and listened to "Alabastor" telling about a girl in Dunedin taking him for someone else, and asking him why he didn't meet her last night. After dinner it came on to rain and blow, and very cold and squally, us 3 and "Alabastor" the 2nd Mate, "Gilpin" "Nimble" and Freeberg, all went out in the boat, and we went away up the harbour to the head of one of the arms. The 2nd Mate and we landed on a little sandy beach, in a little bay and got ferns and broadleaf for the cow, there was such lovely bits of loose sea-weed floating close up to the shore and all such bright colours showing up against the white sand down below. It kept on sharp squalls of rain, and Fannie had on "Alabastors" cloak, and Lillie and I were under Captain's coat. We landed in another little bay, very wee, and all slippery brown rocks covered in slimey sea-weed, all this little rattle seaweed, and directly you stepped on them you slipped and went flying, if you didn't look out. We got more stuff for the cow and "Nimble" got some earth in a bag, and Fannie and I were getting some ferns off a bank and we got bogged getting at them just by the boat, so we told Lillie to get some from there, and she got bogged too, and we laughed at her.

S.S "Hinemoa" ab

Hinemoa at sea.

31st 10/90. from.

When we were at the first little bay Fannie and I both carved on the pine it was only a young tree with a nice straight stem. It came on a heavy hail shower and we could hear it pelting up among the trees, I was carving with my old knife and my hands were freezing to bits. "Gilpin" shot a shag flying away over, a real good shot, and when we said so, he made out it was nothing. "Gilpin" shot another Shag and broke its wing. We saw a lot of shags nests, and a bit of green sea weed stuck on a stick on the bank where the tide goes up to. We had it for a mark to know if we were coming back the right way it was such a bright green and flapping away in the wind.

The green seaweed we used for a marker.

We pulled up to a little clump of manukas on the bank, and "Gilpin" got out and went up to them with his white canvas game bag slung over his back and his gun pointed at them, and went poking all round them with his gun all ready as if he expected to see all the game on earth to fly out, *little owl*!!! As if anything would stay in there with the boat pulling under its nose and us all talking. "Alabastor" and the 2nd. Mate went up to the top of the hill and got some lovely coral moss and gave it to Lillie. We didn't get out of the boat as we were too cold to move, and our feet were soaking wet and *freezing*, and our hands were no better off.

We had a fine pull and we got on board and were late for tea, as well as late for breakfast, and then after tea Lillie practised and Fannie and I tied our legs to-gether and walked up and down the saloon. The twine nearly cut our ankles in two then we tied our same side legs together and our arms and tried to do all sorts of things. We did laugh too, and then we got in the pantry and emptied a bottle of pickels, and I opened a new one and ate half. When I was opening them I sat down backwards on the seat and upset all the vinegar on my green dress. It was dark in there and "Moondyne" was in his cabin, then we ate some salt meat, Lillie finished off the meat when going to bed, the minute we went upstairs, out he came "Moondyne" and yarned away as friendly as possible to "Alabastor", till all hours, and we turned in ending one more day for ever–

Thursday
23rd October 1890

I dreampt of standing on top of a hedge and pressing it down and I thought Ernest wanted us to go to his house and stay with him and we did not want to go, then I woke up.

– Up early, and only just dressed in time for breakfast and we had a beautiful fish, Trumpeter. Very cold and cloudy, and showery every now and then. "Alabastor" and "Nimble" and Freeberg and the 2nd. Mate all went in the dingy up Seal creek. We saw 3 cranes. The first 2 we saw in a little bay and one had a nest away up on top of a high old dead tree. "Alabastor" had a shot at one and missed, he knocked some feathers out of one poor beautiful bird. We were so wild with him because one had a nest and were *delighted* when he didn't get them, he was perched in the bows of the boat and wanted us to keep quiet coming round all the bends and corners but we talked coming to where the cranes were. He shot one tuft shag, and he kept on diving, they wouldn't half look for it, he wounded another and let it get away too *great muff*!!! He shot four Red bills – there were some sitting on a rock poking out of the water.

These are meant for Red-bills please

It seemed so cruel to shoot them with their poor little blue boddies and red bills and legs, we landed and got stuff for the cow, and saw heaps of shags fly out of their nests, when we pulled up in a quiet nook down past the boat. We pulled up under the trees and saw and heard the young shags in the shells singing out and squeeking by the dozen, in the eggs and half out and all kinds of ways. We pulled down the branches of the trees they were leaning right out over the water and looked into the nests, they had heaps of eggs in them and young birds. "Alabastor" got two kinds of shags eggs, and we saw some blue shags but didn't get any. They are good for eating, and we saw a pair of paradise ducks, but they both got away.

The two Seals on the Snares make straight for us - 24.10.90.

Moffet kept on fireing his gun off just over our heads and between our heads and Fannie was wild with him because, it made her ears go funny. He was steering (or thought he was) and let go the steer-oar to fire at a shag, but he said dam – when he missed the shag and then the steer-oar got adrift, – then begged our pardon – we didn't care for that anyway.–

Up at the head of the creek, we saw another crane and they polled the boat along with the handles of the oars, so as not to take a splash pulling and frighten the crane, it settled just ahead of us down behind some trees. The dingy got aground and "Nimble" carried "Alabastor" ashore and bogged in the mud over it. The tide was just about out and he landed Moffet by a big stone, and got some more earth with a tommy up on the bank. Freeberg had to keep shoving the boat off to keep us afloat. "Alabastor" crept thro' the bush and shot the crane. He was quite delighted, it was such a beautiful bird and as white as white. We had to turn back, and we went back to where the two cranes were and got stuff for the cow, and Lillie got "Nimbles" tommy-hawk from him and hacked up a bag full of earth. Coming back there was such a heavy hail squall we pulled under the bank for shelter, and the 2nd. Mate got out and squatted on some rocks right under a ledge of rock for shelter. It was lovely looking at the hail all hopping in the water and dancing about like mad fairys, it did look funny looking along the water from the boat. It came on harder and harder until it made a kind of fust all over the water, with the fine splatters from each hailstone. When it passed off Fannie had a ring of hail all round her neck stuck on the fir of her ulster, and our knees were white and round our necks too and all the boat. Our seats got damp when the hail melted into slush, we got another hail squall so heavy it nearly filled the boat, it was lovely up the creek and we had a fine view of the Frazer Peaks, they are all bare grannet.

We got on board after a very hard pull, about two, and got back late for dinner and had it at 2, and gobbled tarts after it. "Moondyne" had a can of fine hot water waiting for us in our cabin when we came on board and some fine old fluffy towels, good old "Moondyne". We were jolly glad of it too as our hands were just about off, and numb with the cold, they wouldn't do anything– We stayed on board all afternoon, and I practised for an hour and a half, and Lillie planted ferns, then sat reading in the sun by the engine room with Fannie till T, and have T at 5 five, and after it we walked up and down the deck till it got quite dry and our feet wet. 7 sailors were walking up and down forrard, and one fireman in a bright blue jacket, two others were arm in arm. I went down. Lillie and Fannie saw a gap of blue sky showing through the cloud, just like a big oval looking glass, there was a very lovely bright rainbow this evening.

"Alabastor" went to look for the other two cranes in the dingy and so did "Merryeanus", "Gilpin", the 2nd. Mate and "Milk-and-water" and a lot from aft all went looking for the cranes. I copied "Frazer Peaks" there are 3 of them, we are still anchored at Port Pegasus.

They all came back without anything, we were awful glad they didn't get the cranes. It is a most beautiful moonlight night, the wind has gone round to the South so we will likely get fine weather now. When we were in the boat today after one of the hail squalls, "Alabastor" told Fannie to put her hand out, she did, and he rubbed hail all over it. We practised, and "Moondyne" and I had a game of draughts, and then Fannie and I had, and then Fannie and "Alabastor" and he and "Moondyne' all had a try. Us 3 and those two men had an arguement about girls and we ran down the girls right and left. We went up to bunk and we danced jigs and had "15 men on the dead mans chest" in our cabin and had grand fun till late, and we turned in and slept not, for the mad rolling.

81

(and again its ____)

Sunday Dec 6th 1891

Lillie, Ethel, & Fannie get upset when out boating, & hoist a signal of distress

Ethel R.

Friday

24th October 1890

We left Port Pegasus at twelve in the night, and got to the Snares (four hundred seventy feet) at breakfast time, and landed after breakfast, and "Moondyne," "Nimble," "Merryeanus", and Martin and "Hard-at-it" and "Alabastor" Freeberg and us three and Captain and the second mate all went in the big boat.

It was very rough getting into the boat. Just as I was getting in the "Hinemoa" rolled away from the boat and down went the boat and up she came on the next wave and the "Hinemoa" rolled to meet her and drove the gangway through one of the thwarts and smashed it. Part of the gangway broke and I got my thumb jambed between the iron and wood, it was jolly sore too, all my nail went black.

We pulled through a big cave, it was very high and a good distance through, it was lovely in there, and when we were right in, the light from the other end lit up all the boat and all hands in her and seemed quite white against the black inky looking water. I shall always remember them as I saw them then, it looked so pretty and I wont forget it ever.– we were the first girls to ever go on the Snares and in the other big cave, Moffet said it aught to be called the "Elf Cave" (E.L.F.) – only our initials are rong Lillie's should be first – as we were the first girls to go in.

When we were through the first cave we landed Martin and "Hard-at-it" to cut grass for the cow, and then went into another cave and it was all water dripping and running down at the mouth and all ran in the boat and on us. We went a long way back to the ledge of rock where the seals are, and it was quite dark and far in, and very high and big. Some one lit a match and it looked like a fusty spot in the great empty cave and never showed a thing, it was downright ghostly in there, no sound but the waves gurgling and coiling up in the black cracks.

rls to go in, when we got through the first ca

landed martin & "Hard-at-it to cut grass fo

cow, & then went into another cave, & it wa

We came out and landed, and saw 3 fir seals getting up on the rocks, one big one and two smaller, one got in the water and the other two came at us, they did snort and glare. Captain threw the axe at one to drive it away– they were right in our road – and cut the side of its head, such a gash poor beggar, we were half scared at them they seemed so vicious. We landed two kiwis, two possoms, and two goats, a mother and young one, and saw all the penguins by the dozen, all sitting in hundreds in patches where it was very wet and muddy and the eggs were very dirty. They got two buckets of penguin eggs. We came back to the boat and went up into the boat harbour to land the goats possoms and kiwis, they just opened the door of the possoms cage and left them to come out when they liked. We saw 7 other goats on the Island, and can't they go over the rocks.

The Island is nearly all bush and in the open places is covered with coarse grass, and the penguins are *just in hundreds*. The 3 seals we saw always live in the boat harbor. Then we pulled back and got Martin and "Hard-at-it" Captain was wild with them when he saw how little grass they only had. They were sitting waiting when we got there and their bags not full, and Captain asked them "if they had been asleep?" because they had cut so little. "Alabastor" shot a dear little black Tomtit, all pure black but with a wee speck of white on each wing. "Nimble" had to jump ashore and go for it, and couldn't find it for a long time, first he went too high then too low, and too much to one side, then the other and Captain was wild and kept on yelling at him, and said *"at your nose Peterson, at your nose"*.

85

We went through the cave again, and it came on to rain very heavy and we hung about under the lee of the Island and waited for the "Hinemoa" to steam in closer, it was miles too rough out there for us to get along side. Captain told the Mate to steam in when he saw us coming off, and he didn't, the rain was pelting down when we were waiting and Fannie only had a jacket and no ulster and "Moondyne" took the clean bag Charlie had over him and put it over her knees, and poor little Charlie had to put on a dirty one. There were such heaps of little stormy petrels all flying down low on the top of the water and diving under it and so close to the boat, and Captain was wild with the mate because he didn't bring the "Hinemoa" in close, and it was too rough to go far out, he waved his hat and scooped in the air with it (pouring rain all the time) and kept on "why ever doesn't that stoopid owl come in I wonder?" and when he found he didn't come he said "oh come on, I suppose we'll have to pull half way to the Auckland Islands for him".

Going on board Lillie slipped and all most fell into the sea, the boat sunk away from under her just as she was half way onto the gangway, it was awfully rough and Lillie would have been in only for the 2nd. Mate and Fannie pushing her up. Fannie's legs flew out from under her and she slipped down and caught her chin against the gunnal. Got on board again and left before 11 for the Auckland Islands, and rather rough, I copied the Snares, and I dreampt last night of something and forgot it and so I will not write down what I cannot remember. Just now as I write, "Moondyne" is lying down on the setee, looking as if he didn't feel as nice as he might, and it was rough, and I went to sleep nearly on the setee. Lillie and Fannie shut "Merryeanus" in the bath room and the Oyster fireman ("Once-a-week") gave them a stick to put in the ring of the door, and they held him fine and firm. – In the afternoon Lillie was rather rum, and came not to T, and after T, Lillie and Fannie stood on the stairs for a bit, and we looked at the lovely sunset over the sea,and watched the Albatross and lovely little cape pidgeons flying round. Spray was coming over every bit of the ships forrard and aft, then Lillie and Fannie went and stood near the engine room and listened to Walter, that's "Milk-and-water" playing the according, and I helped " Moondyne" clean penguins eggs, 12 of them. After, "Merryeanus" came down into the saloon, and grabbed Fannie sitting by the fire and gave her such a scrubbing (hang the man) and Fannie and I played draughts, and went in the cabin opposite the pantry and ate the ham and got caught at it too, and turn we in at 10.

Saturday

25th October 1890

Up early, and find ourselves at the Auckland Islands, at day light, in Port Ross, the boat went ashore with Captain and "Alabastor" and "Merryeanus", we saw it out our port-holes when we were almost dressed, and we were so wild because they didn't wait for us, and they wouldn't go again so we didn't get.

They looked at the depot and everything all right. Yesterday "Gilpin" shot a *white Nellie*, and a Mollyhawk, they were two lovely birds, he was so over joyed over it he was quite jolly to us and gabbled away at the rate of knots the whole day – he shot the white Nellie off the Snares. We moved down from Port Ross before breakfast, to the mouth of the harbor.

We are looking out for a place to christen *"Mt Chow Chuckle"* the highest and most jaggy place we can see, but we must go up to the top of it to name it. Then we steamed down to Enderby Island and anchored. Captain, "Alabastor", and "Merryeanus" and "Gilpin" and Charlie, came with us on shore "Alabastor" and "Gilpin" had their guns to shoot rabbits, we saw them on shore from off the vessel hopping around by dozens almost all black and silver grey, they are very shy, directly we got ashore they were all gone. We took two goats an old and a young and a Southdown sheep and let them go ashore, but the poor old beggars wouldn't leave the boat and stopped on the beach by it.

Trying to get the goat along Enderby beach. Sat 25/10/90.

One of the "Derry Castle" huts.

We all chivied them and tryed to pull the old goat along by her horns but she stuck her feet in the sand and wouldn't budge, Captain wanted to get them over the sand hill to where the other sheep were. We were so cold we ran up and down the sand hill, and even then we were blue with the cold, we got some Albatross bones on the sand so clean and white, and then went along to the boat shed. We chased 4 sealions into the sea two yellow and two dark, the first three we saw were just on the short grass above the sand and we ran straight up to them and we 3 chased the sealions, they kept coming at us, one snorted and came at Fannie and she hopped away and said *"Oh! shut up."* We had *grand fun* after them, and ran the 3 down to the water, and we could hear them on board laughing at us. Then we went up and looked at the "Derry Castle" huts, they were made of tussock and sticks tied together with strips of sea lions skin, Lillie got some bits to keep, we went in one of the huts, you had to crawl in Lillie got some moss from the roof of one of the huts just a little dump, it was so dry inside too, the "Derry Castle" crew built the huts, 3 of them, and lived in them 22 months when they were wrecked there.

"Merryeanus" shot a Sparrow Hawk and wounded another it got away in some vinegar plant. We helped hunt for it and I hid his tommy hawk, and Fannie put his cap in an old iron can of water, and he paid Lillie out for it, then Fannie took his handkerchief and told him it was hidden and sent him to look for it. We went up and looked at the boat shed and Captain got Lillie some plant, that was growing there, then he and "Merryeanus" went on board again. We saw 3 wingless Snipe an old one and two young ones, I caught one in the long grass, such a dear little brown wretch, and let it go again, they were so pretty and had no wings and little or no tail, and a very long beak a bill more like this.

Three wingless Snipe.

It was *freezing cold* and came on to rain, so we went up by the boat shed and sat in the vinegar shrubs for shelter, and sang *"They all love Jack"* and looked at the Sea hens flying around, they are brown and jolly big. We did not get much shelter from the rain and our seats were rather on the damp side, the fern was wet. We spied a yellow sea-lion a jolly big one sitting on the sand away at the other end of the beach and stretching its neck out of joint listening to "Alabastor" and "Gilpin" shooting, so we started and ran for it, and when we were running along the beach after it I caught my foot in a coil of kelp and fell full length flat out in the creek, and smashed all my Albertross bones except one wishing bone and all the water ran up my sleeves.

I yelled out to Lillie to run on, then got up and picked up my only whole bone left, and ran on too, we ran and ran but the sand was heavy and we had a long way to go, Lillie was just about 10 steps away when it got to the edge of the water and she was too limp to run any more, it was in such a hurry to dive into the water it dived into the sand, and we never got it, it made such a splash getting in, and we got half way along the beach before it saw us, and then it floundered down through the sand and made such a track. We hunted in the grass for more and heard them snorting and when we were running after one Fannie tripped and fell on an Albatross beak she was carrying and broke it against her eyebrow, it jolly nearly went in her eye too. The sea lions have a very lacadasical look when they are sitting still, and they have lovely big eyes and tears always running down their cheeks. We saw the sheep and two goats lying down together, they seem such good friends regular old chums. When we lost the sea lion we went up to the bush and got shelter as it was raining hard, we got under a thick scrub, and there was a mockingbird hopping about in the scrub, and such lovely soil for flowers under the trees, then we came down to the beach so they would see us and send the boat off. We threw big stones in the water under the bank and stood on them for shelter, we had our dresses turned up over our heads to keep us dry, and waited for the boat to come off.

Waiting for the boat. Enderby Island

"Alabastor" and "Gilpin" got heaps of rabbits 11 all black colour, "Gilpin" said "have the young ladies gone off yet?" and we were under the rocks for shelter and he never saw us. The boat came off for us with "Hard-at-it" and the 1st. Mate and our ulsters, we said we expected they trailed them after the boat inside-out. "Gilpin" wanted to shoot a little sand lark that was running about by us, he said "where is it Miss Richardson?" and we said *"there – there it goes"* and we pointed along the beach, and all the time it was just down behind his legs, and he never saw it, and it got away. He was wexed because he couldn't stay and get more rabbits, we saw a lot of sand larks on shore they are pretty little beggars and nearly the colour of the sand and you can hardly see them running on the sand. When we were putting off in the boat we saw a little wingless duck swimming over the kelp, it is like a teal and very uncommon so of course "Alabastor" wanted it at once, he was getting all the different kinds of birds he could and he and "Gilpin" fired 5 shots at it poor little beggar before they could kill it, every time they fired it would dive, in among the kelp, and it was just the colour of kelp and we got it. Came on board and still raining, We left about 12, and came down the East coast to Carnley Harbour and got in about 5., After dinner we coiled up in the saloon and tried to go to sleep, far too much rolling for that though, but I nearly went to sleep on the way from Enderby Island to Carnley Harbour. "Moondyne" woke me with a bit of a hawk's wing tickling me on the face and Moffet told him to do it because I heard him, he was sitting by the stove. It was pouring and blowing great guns, and a terrible beam sea and poor "Nimble" was heaving coal aft on the weather side all day. It was very rough coming up the harbour, we saw one hut or depot but it was too rough to think of landing. Fannie asked the Oyster fireman "if the engines were stopped?" he said "they're just going over the centre" and Fannie said "Yes, I knew they were". We chose *"Mt Chow Chuckle"* plenty of jaggy rocks and not much climbing to get up.

And here we are anchored for the night and blowing like fun and raining, we can see "Fairchilds Garden" from the port, and this is a fine big harbour and a little like Wellington in the rain, there is hardly anything growing near the water but thick sea – veronicar. We had some of the rabbits for T and they were just *scrumptious*, but at the same time it was full of chopped up bones (the stew was) It is raining *hard* and pouring and *how* the wind *howls*, and the glass is down to 28, 64. and still falling and although in a sheltered spot Captain has let go both anchors and is keeping up steam in case we drag in the night and have to take to our heels and clear. Fannie and I sat by the fire, and "Moondyne" is in the pantry scraping eggs and "Alabastor" is drawing ("*things like dishcovers*" Lillie said) *ment* for sketches of the "Derry Castle" huts and there is a ring of wet boots round the fire, sticking up all round the stove, just now from running through the wet grass after sea lions.

It is two months to Xmas, and I wonder what we will be doing this date a month and two months ahead? *who knows*? "Moondyne" was telling of the smuggling, and was playing draughts with "Alabastor" with my draught board, and Lillie and I were going to drop candle grease on their heads if they lost the game, turned in at 10, I did not turn in till 12 I was washing, and fixing up things, I washed my head and nearly froze my head off, the water was *freezing* – and *cold, rather* so, it *was*. So ends another day and a jolly good day we had boys!! – "And at length this happy day, Like a passion died away"–

NOT TRUE.

I WISH IT HAD BEEN.

"Camped out", Bluff beach.

New Zealand. E. Shell.

Sunday
26th October 1890

Up early, and very cold, and snow close down on the hills all round, we were anchored in Carnely Harbour still, and soon after breakfast we landed, and went sea-lion hunting, there were sixteen of us came off in the dingy, we had fine fun after the sealions.

The first one was very vicious and got away every time they put a noose over its head, we were after it down on the flat sort of bit by the creek, and we caught 2 sea lions. One was such a big one and dark brown, it got so vicious we got up under a bank out of the way, it flew after the men and went for "Gilpin" who ran for bare life and fell in a hole and Mr Miller was running away too and fell in one of these deep sort of ditch places all sloppy brown swamp mud, we roared laughing from our perch. *Oh! misery it was cold.*

It came on to blow hard, then poured with rain the water was running off our faces and noses and off the peaks of our caps, we laughed at the cut of ourselves, we were all a little apart. It hailed and came on to sleet and snowed in turns, and we were nigh frozen our feet were like lumps of lead.

We had enough of staying still, so we made tracks up the hill and soon got warmer. We brought a sheep ashore and let it go, they caught the sea lion in the end and put it in the boat under the thwarts and tied it there, "Hard-at-it" was left in charge of it, the first sea lion they didn't catch, it was the second we tracked and got him and put him in the boat he was very vicious too, but not so bad as the first who escaped into the water. When we were going ashore to Adams Isle the sea lions swam after us and popped their heads out of the water and snorted at us, Charlie was half scared of them, and we went up the hill after another one, and we were only half way up the hill when "Hard-at-it' began to yell out and wave his arms because a sea lion was coming down near the boat, and some were snorting at him out of the water, so Captain sent "Gilpin" look after it.

"position is everything", when you want to scare an enemy.

Position is everything when you want to scare an enemy

"Legs are everything" when an enemy scares you.

Legs are everything when an enemy scares you

Lillie and I went right to the top of the hill, and looked out over the cliff which hung out over the sea. Moffet came up and shot about 12 lovely shags, but only got two as the others fell into the sea, it was such a waste to shoot the lovely birds and let them fall over the cliff into the sea, they were so lovely and had such lovely green necks and such white feathers. They got another sea lion up the side of the hill, but it tore the bags to pieces and nearly got away, so Captain and Noberry and "Gilpin" and Miller all went back to the "Hinemoa", and took the first one off and left the Carpenter and 2nd. Mate to look after the sea lion, and us 3 stopped while the boat got fresh gear. The sea lion did wriggle like old boots, I saw 30 when the gun went off, all at once stretching their necks out of the grass to listen to Moffet fireing. I went up and poked the sea lion through a hole in the bag, and I wanted to sit on it, it had its head in a bag, but "Merryeanus" said don't because it might get away. I was throwing those carroty sort of leaves at two that were asleep across a ditch sort of place so I got into the sort of ditch for a few stones that were there, and I looked up and one small one close to me made for me, and was almost at me, and I was in such a scare because Captain said if they caught you they would hang on till they shook you to bits, and in my hurry to turn and run I fell down– lord I thort I was caught. I looked round as I crawled and clawed up the bank and the sea-lion had just stopped, thank goodness for me, I kept my stones tho' and hit it on the nose too, and made it shake its head, then they both went off down the hill. Captain said the nose is the tenderest place to hit them on, and we chased heaps of them, they came back and took the last one on board, and we went along the beach and got wee pawas while the boat went to Monumental Island.

95

We laughed at the cut of ourselves.

I nearly ran against a sea lion along the beach, I was just walking along a narrow strip of beach with a skull I found and Fannie called out "look around" and I did, and there was a sea lion close to my face glaring at me on the bank, it could have grabbed me if it liked, and Lillie and Fannie had to come past it too. And the darned old "Oger" banged a poor sea lion so hard that he broke his stick, and Paget scolded him even. We went up on top of the hill and watched "Nimble" after some sea lions he was in delight and showing off awfully, and throwing a tree at one. We found a monster big sea lion and routed him out, we tried to drive him down the hill but lost him in the scrub Pat went after him and lost his hat. We found lovely purple veronicar up on the hill and I found a kind of forget me-not, as well as some veronicar.

Fannie routed out a sea lion that went floundering off down over a steep bank, and she went sliding down after it nearly all knickerbockers, and chased it into the sea, and we slid down after Fannie only not in such a hurry. We were playing with them down by the water, we saw heaps of them in the water and they did snort at us, there were a lot over by the bank coiled up to-gether asleep. I got two skulls, and all the hills were covered in snow, and it was cold. Lillie had a wingless snipe to hold for "Merryeanus" in his old red handkerchief, and she opened the top to see if it had enough air and it hopped out and away, but Lillie got it again, she got such a scare she thought it was off. "Alabastor" killed a sea lion with 4 shots he wanted its head (Captain was away in the boat.) The *horrid* old "Oger" cut its head off before it was properly dead, it had such black meat, and had a big hole in its side where the 4 charges went in you could see all its lungs, *cruel beggars* the poor sea lion galloped too, to try and save itself. We went aboard and had dinner about 2. We went to the depot and boat shed, and stopped and the dingy went ashore.

Fannie after a Sea Lion.
on Adams Island Sun/26/10/90.

93.

Looking over a cliff on Adams Island

We left Adams Island after dinner, and it was just cold. We are off again down the strait, to the remains of the "Grafton" we saw two pigs on the beach as we were pulling off to the shore, one was a skinny yellow, and instead of pulling to luard of the pigs and getting into the bush and sneaking down behind them, "Gilpin" was so eager to shoot them like an owl he made them pull strait at them and of course they made off into the bush as hard as they could, and that was the last they saw of them and serve them right for being such apes, they must have known better. We landed where the "Grafton" was wrecked and walked over her, and I got some of her I broke it off myself, and saw the place where the men off her were for 20 months, and saw the remains of Musgroves hut and stove, I put my name under the supporting bit of wood and on the main bit, it was in pencil, pressed in hard, and I scratched it with my knife on two bits of copper, and on top of this pole was a cross board and written on it was (HMS "Blanche" July 1870.), and there was another notice, and on it was (made provisions good, May 5th. 1879, HMS "Emerald".) Charlie got Lillie some moss off one of the poles of the hut, it was a round clump growing right at the top, Lillie asked him to get it as she couldn't reach it, he had to clime up for it.

And the big Sea Lion finds us!
Adams Island Sun/26/10/90.

30/6/93
E

Adams Island

We saw one sea lion, and it was cold, we came on board, and off out to sea with a low glass and a furious freezing wind, and a frantic beam sea we left for the Campbell Islands then and it was rough and we turned in early, and I could not sleep. I heard a pencil in one of the drawers rolling backwards and forwards I was so wild with it and wouldn't get up and stop it. It kept on roll, roll roll– *clack*, up against one side, then roll, roll roll, clack up against the other side, I could have nearly eaten that pencil, and I thought oh you *brute* if I get out I'll teach you to roll, and I had to get out of bunk in the end and stop it, but the "Hinemoa" did roll, violin and all I could hardly stick in–

"Rolling, rolling over the stormy deep,
Many a night I've lain awake
Without a wink of sleep.

99

Monday
27th October 1890

Got up and it was rough, we could not sleep all night we rolled so much, Lillie nearly got banged to atoms dressing.

We got to Monumental Bay about half past 8, we only stayed a few minutes then on, and had our breakfast at 10, and we wanted to land there and go up to the snow, we got to the Campbell Isds. at 9 or from half past 8 to 9 somewhere. We had breakfast on our way round to "Nor West Bay" or "Penguin Harbour" and we saw just thousands of Molly hawks on the cliffs they were sitting, and gulls and Albatrosses flying in great circles round and round, with their lovely big white white wings.

As soon as we anchored in "Nor West Harbour" they put two sheep and two goats ashore, then came back and took us 3 and "Alabastor" and "Merryeanus" the 2nd. Mate and "Moondyne" ashore about 11 and we went up the hills to the snow. It was a rough climb and cold, going up the hill Fannie and I made old "Merryeanus" pull us up a bit, and then he hauled Lillie up a bit she was so out of puff she could hardly get up, and up on top "Merryeanus" got Lillie some rare plants. Moffet wasn't on for such a rough climb and he stopped poking about where the boat landed us, planting acorns, as if oaks would grow there. "Moondyne" stopped on top with an Albertross he killed, and "Merryeanus" with another. "Alabastor" (gave it up) like the "Frate caravan Horse" at the top of the hill, and went back to his beloved oak planting and us 3 and the 2nd. Mate went on up through the snow till we saw the depot house up Perseverance Harbour, and the bay we were in this morning, and right down Perseverance harbor. We could see most of the Island, and the sea nearly all round, for miles, and we saw heaps of young Albertrosses up on top sitting in their nests all among the snow, they were so lovely and clean and soft looking.

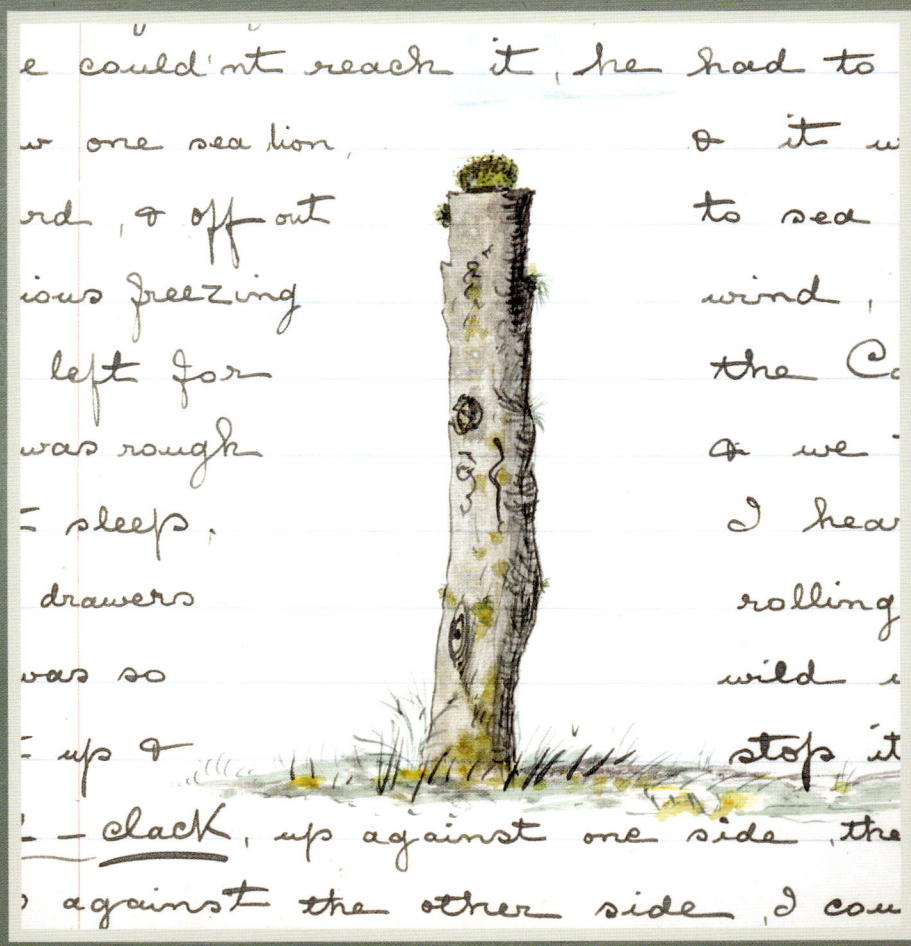

Charlie got Lillie some moss of a pole.

There were such funny plants up there and all grassy stuff and sort of slipped in places all soft earth and rather muddy, the only trees there are in the gullys they have been blown to bits anywhere except in the gullys, and all the tops clipped off flat with the bitter cold wind. When we went to get some of our biscuits out of our pockets to eat our hands were so cold we could not get them out, our hands were quite numb and wouldn't do anything, we ate a good lot of snow but it was so cold it made our teeth ache. It came on to rain heavy and it did just rain, and blow, the 2nd. mate showed us where a French middie off a Man-o-war is buried, they came here to watch the transet of venus.

Every two or three minutes one of us will fall.

It was so cold we didn't know what to do especially when we faced the wind coming back, we turned to come down the hill again at half past 12, Lillie put her ulster on when it came on to rain, the 2nd. mate carried it for her up the hill and along the top, and carried it through a strap he had round his waist to have his hands free, Fannie had on her jacket and I had nothing, so I had the tail of Lillies ulster round me to try and keep my top half dry.

We were soaking up past our knees from the wet tussocky stuff and snow, and it was hard to keep together every two or three minutes one of us would fall and I trod on Lillie's dress many times and tore it out of the pleets at the top. All most every step one of us would go to our knees Lillie was wild with me and she *did swear* because I trod on her dress, and I left her and ran down the hill, we collected up along at the top and we 3 got behind all the men because we were nearly all knickerbockers the wind was blowing our dresses up so, and we were all of us singing "When Jonny comes marching home, *hurrah!!! hurrah!!!!*"

And it was pouring cats and dogs all the while. "Merryeanus" and "Moondyne" got a good many birds and "Marryeanus" had two big live Albertrosses one under each arm, and we roared at him doing his best to come down the hill decently, he fell and had no arms to save himself and rolled over heaps of times. We all fell coming down and I got bogged in slouchy swamp mud close to the bottom of the hill, I ran right into it.

Lillie got some stag-horn moss and some other stuff something like it. "Alabastor" stayed looking for the blue veronicar down near the water and never got any and we got some on top, he wished he'd gone right up then.

102

We were just about pulp we were so wet, Lillie walked into the water to get the dirt out of her dress, we were wet to the skin, the Mate came off with the boat for us and we got on board like drowned rats, we were just wet through. We got back about half past 2, Lillie and Fannie squeezed the water out of their skirts on deck and Lillie's ulster was just as wet inside as out.

We skinned and changed from head to toe, poor old Captain was quite alarmed because we were so wet. We had dinner at nearly 4 p.m. and the tea at the ordinary time, no wonder we went hungry, and no wonder we *were hungry* at dinner. After it Lillie sorted up her moss and plants till tea we went around to Perseverance harbour after dinner and anchored for the night. We passed Blanche rock on our way and "Gilpin" was wild because he could not land and get some Molly hawks eggs, they were just in scrawms on the cliffs sitting. "Moondyne" covered me in cushions, I was sitting in the corner, so Fannie and I went into the fidley and sowed up his pockets, his pants were hanging in there to dry, our dresses had to be put in the fidley too to dry.

The glass is falling, after tea "Gilpin" and "Alabastor" and others went up the harbour and got some flint, and gave us some. Lillie and I reefed up all "Moondyne's" bed clothes then put on two of his ties and gave ourselves each a cigarette of blotting paper and waited for him to see us. We practised, and we 3 went into the pantry and ate ham and pickles, and went off up to bunk early, as it is very cold and we have both anchors down as it is blowing great guns, we turned in early and slept, sound, sound and...

"High aloft amongst the rigging sings the loud exulting gale"

103

In the snow!
Campbell Islands.

the snow! Campbell Islands.
28/10/910.

Wading out to the boat at Cape Campbell Island.

Tuesday

28th October 1890

I dreampt of being in front of the stables at "Oaklands" and "Gilpin"...

...was there with two overcoats on and all undone down the front and it was raining like old boots, and he kept on putting out his hand to see if it was raining and I thought he was tite and we were sorry, then I thought I was getting a cup full of cocoa out of a bath full what was for the hands, and then Fannie and I were tying up some ones shoe strings and then I was making my horse gallop across the lawn, and I was in my singlet and knickerbockers, and old Stevens from Jacksons Bay came walking up the drive and asked me "if Pa was in?" I said "yes," and he knew it was me, and then Pa and he came walking down the old path, and Pa saw me run behind the clump and I was afraid because of my rig and got thro' where we used to jump the fence and crawled into a bunch of broom and found Fannie there and we crawled out thro' the little old gate and there was old Stevens getting through after me and Pa comming to catch me the other way and he had on a white hat and oilskin and he called me and was angry because Fannie and I had tied up the laces – and then I woke and slept and dreampt again of all the leburnum being out in blossom the dear old gold blossom – I woke – and got up and we were still anchored in Perseverance harbor. Rough outside too rough to go on, and very cold and showery all morning.

Before dinner we practised and Lillie planted her flowers, and after dinner "Moondyne" came down and asked if they could have the boat to go ashore, we couldn't deside whether to go in the boat or not it was so cold and blowing hard, and "Moondyne" didn't want us to go, and Moffet backed out of it and martyrised by the saloon fire making miserys with Captain over being kept by the bad weather. We asked "Merryeanus" out by the fidley if we should come and that the others didn't want us to go, he said "yes come and never mind the others" he was the only one who wanted us to come (good old friend when the others were grumpy) At last we went, in the dingy, "Moondyne" "Merryeanus" 1st. Mate and "Milk-and-water" and "Hard-at-it" and Miller and the other engineer, all were going after Albertrosses and did not want us to come, but we *did* come, and landed up by the sailors grave, and they all went off as hard as they could peg up the hill Albertrossing, but us 3 and "Merryeanus" stayed to dig worms for his snipe.

In the old hut on the Campbell Islands.

We went in the old sealers or whalers hut. "Merryeanus" carved something up over the door, and we looked for the middies grave. Then we got in the boat and I pulled, and we went up and we got out at the top of the bay, we pulled under a bank for shelter and Lillie steered with an oar and then on up "Merryeanus" got worms, and we got grass for the cow, and punui.

Then we pulled over to the other side where they got the trancet of venus, but didn't land and came back and landed. The tide went down so quick the dingy was dry in two minutes "Merryeanus" told me to push her off and so I gave her a shove off and slipped in and got my feet wet, then hauled her up and made fast, "Merryeanus" was laughing at me trying to push her off, it was all very fine for him. We got in the dingy and I steered with an oar and we pulled down and landed at the point and found the "Middies" grave and it had an iron cross on it and some stone on top, I copied the cross onto a bit of the stone in pencil and gave it to Lillie, it was a sort of chalk stone, it is a pretty cross and we left the grave and came out the broad track that had been cut to carry the poor middie to his lonely grave – we went to the edge of the bank and sat under the trees as it was raining again. It kept on raining then the sun came out for a few minutes and the dingy looked so pretty when the sun shone out all over her and on the little sandy beach with all the green punui heaped up in her bows she was half in the water and half out, I will *always* remember her –

awn I landed at the point I found the "middies" grav
I it had an
iron cross on
some stone on top. I copied the cross on to a bit of
he stone in pencil I gave it to Lillie. it was a sort of

I will never forget how the dingy looked.

"Merryeanus" and Fannie were at it, and I did laugh, Fannie offered him a dead sand fly, and when he went to pay her out, she said "O! look out for my arm its twisted" and "take care you are tearing my dress" and all sorts of excuses "look out because I'm just opening my knife", Lillie and I had such fun laughing at them. We had got under the scrub from the rain, I got more punui there for the cow.

"Merryeanus" said *"we'd would be three inches nearer Heaven"* for taking the trouble to get the stuff for the cow, he was up on the bank digging down a tussock and "mercy he's had his time too" and he laughed at us because we said the dead fizzy stuff off the inaka trees would make nice cat's nests, he said "it was such a funny thing to think of" so it would too. We got in the dingy and pulled round another point and up another bay, and we saw 3 sheep near the edge of the scrub. Then it was 10 after 5 and we went back to the "Hinemoa", and I was steering still, and quite proud of myself and the rest of us pulling, we had fine fun, I brought the boat along side fine style, Captain did not see us coming and asked "who brought the boat back?" we said *"we did"*, "what did the carpenter do?" we told him he was pulling too. We had T and after T "Merryeanus" and the 2nd. Mate went back for the others, and took them a *big can of hot tea rolled up to keep warm, (you bet they take good care of the men)* and got them.

We planted things, and looked at the sea lions, and fed the cow, Noberry is the only one of the hands we've seen today, it's a union holiday. Fannie and I got "Gilpin" to let us have a pot at some gulls and did not kill any, the gun kicked so it knocked Fannie's cap on to her nose, she had 5 shots and one time into a bunch of seagulls too. I had a shot and missed, and "Gilpin" had a shot and of course killed his game, and of course smiled accordingly. Fannie hit "Merryeanus" on the nose with a punui leaf when he was in the fidley, and dabbed him with those carroty leaves, he said he would pay her out 6 times for it.

The iron cross on the "Middies" grave.

Moffet is so greedy he has been along again to the meat safe to see how it is lasting, he hates the idea of salt meat. I like it and hope we have nothing else for days, (*men are greedy*) he dos'nt find it too cold to go there every day, he does nothing but molly coddle round the fire and poking Captain up to go, and thinks of nothing but his beloved *meat.* Some of them caught a rat and threw it overboard and "Milk-and-water" cruel old beggar threw potatos at it when it was swimming along side, poor rat was trying to get up everywhere, Fannie and I scolded him as hard as we could. After he was in the pantry talking to "Moondyne" and he was talking about the rough travelling, (and no doubt it was as smooth as a pan-cake,) and talking about the cliffs (if we saw them I suppose they would be fine little banks just high enough to sit on) We saw some goats going along the beach this evening, the glass is rising again, we practised, and we get vicious because, we must go back. We turn in early at 11 I think, and grumpy, grumpy, grumpy. And go to sleep, and we are still anchored in Perseverance Bay and stay for the night. The 3 of us in a row in our bunks fast asleep.

HERE WE ARE AGAIN. L.E. & F.

WE THREE.

Wednesday
29th October 1890

Wake up and find ourselves still anchored with two anchors, up very early and have breakfast, and heave both anchors up and away befor eight. then go from the firthest south we have ever been and from Perseverance Bay and from the Campbell Island.

We sat on deck all morning and a wave came on board and we nearly got wet.

Most frantically cold going down the harbour, we sat on deck singing all sorts of things and looking at Campbell Islands (called after Robert Campbell, a whaler who discovered them in 1810 on the "Sydney".) We are only a mile and a half or degree and a half or something above the Horn, or North of it. It is a fine day only big waves, when we were on deck this morning a big wave came over on to the bridge and soused all the deck, but we escaped by hoisting our legs sky high.

Moffet was enjoying a sleep on the other seat and a big roller came and rolled him on to the deck, "Jove" he said and got up. After dinner we sat on deck again 4 miles out to sea we could see the knob they went by for Albertrosses and the rocks sticking up (Lyall Pyramid) where we went and the 2nd. Mate, we had the topsail, and jib, and staysail set all day but in spite of them we have been rolling about like old boots.

After dinner as usual Moffet molly coddled aft and we 3 sat on deck till T time, it was warm in the sun (and we taught the 2nd. Mate in no time "aye") we asked him to translate the maori for Fannie, and the words that "Merryeanus" gave her. He did and became quite friendly, *eh*! and one of the words ment love (aroha) at the end, I forget the rest. He told of being at all the South sea Islands and in Maritius, every now and then he went and stood forrard, then came back for a few minutes yarn *eh!* Fannie showed him her photo, he said "he couldn't help but know it," at the same time he never guessed who it was. We showed it to "Merryeanus", and he showed us one of him when he was on the "Westland", more like Jack Kydd than anyone else, and another of him in uniform two years ago, and an awful fright it is too. The 2nd. Mate used to be on the brigantine "Oamaru" and he lent Lillie a book of Maori legends. "Merryeanus" gave his Snipe so many worms that it died from the effect. It is very cold this evening and bright moonlight, and away fade the old Campbells, I wonder shall we ever see them again?–

"No bitter dirge from the stormy flow
Of moaning sea,– oh no,no,no,!
But a sweet farewell, and a low soft hynm
Under the beautiful moons that swim
Over the silver seas that toss
Their foam to thy shrine, O Southern Cross."

(O! silent stars, O silver bars of moonlight on this angry sea –)

After tea I played on the piano and wrote I this. When shall we see the Campbell Islands again? We have seen the last of them for a bit. Fannie and I, and "Alabastor" and, I and "Moondyne" and I, had draughts, and we turned in early and slept and it was rough I can tell you, and she did roll and Billie no likey the rolling and never will…

Thursday
30th October 1890

Woke up and found ourselves out at sea and rolling like old boots, we rolled about too much for Lillie to sleep. Up early, and it was very rough and cold, and blowing a hurrican it is far rougher than last night, and cold and seas coming over all the time and after breakfast I sat on the setee till dinner and it was just cold.

We all sat in the saloon most of the day trying to get warm. A big sea came over the galley and soaked Arthur, and after dinner I got my ulster and had a snoose in it all afternoon and I was warm. "Moondyne" woke me up with a bird's wing and "Alabastor" told him to and Lillie was half the afternoon by me rolled up in her ulster. After T "Alabastor" and I had a lot of games of draughts and he and "Moondyne" had and "Moondyne" and I had one and I bet 9 pence and lost. Lillie and Fannie started and talked to "Merryeanus" and he told us of being in Maririus and heaps of places lucky old devil. He said he would come and steal our fruit if we were 3 old maids, he would call his old shipmate to help and they wouldn't be a bit scared of 3 old maids, he said we would not need anything but 3 old cats and a parrot each, and he told us how he sold everything belonging to the sea and went and lived away behind the mountains to get away from it, but soon came back and joined the "Hinemoa" in Wellington. We came down and Lillie and Fannie found the ham behind the pantry door and ate as much as we wanted of it. We all ate biscuits, and we turned in at 10 still very rough and cold and slept I till morning. ("Thou hast our little lives within Thy hands!")–

The thunders and the tempests of the sea,

Changing the narrow limits of the lands–

Friday
31st October 1890

"Moondyne" woke us up and we found ourselves lying too somewhere in hale of the Antipodes and waiting for an observation and for the fog to clear and the "Hinemoa" was rolling about like a tite monkey.

Walking over the Antipodes

It was still very cold but fine, Lillie mended her dress this morning, still rolling about like a cork in a tub of water, we looked at the lovely blue of the waves as they passed the port hole. Next went and fixed up our cabin a bit, it was in an awful mess everything on the floor flying in the wrong direction. Hove to yet and waiting for observations before we can go on. Lillie and Fannie walked up and down a long time and were looking at Captain and the two mates trying to nab the sun and Moffet was on the stairs calling out the time, at last they got the sun and we got an observation and were 20 miles from the Antipodes and that was at 12. After a few minutes we left for the Island just as dinner was ready, and got there about 4.

Pat asked Fannie what would do Charlie good as he was sick, and she said give him a dose of paint. "Nimble" went onto the fidley, and Pat said to Fannie "here's the boy for you – the one who looks through the button hole of his oilskin" and Fannie said "I don't know who you mean" and Pat said "oh you know the one fine you don't kneed me to tell you" and after a bit he said to "Nimble", "why don't you come out?" then he said to Fannie "he's afraid to come out while you're here" he scared "Nimble" so much he opened the fidley door on the weather side and came up on to the bridge that way. I got two boards from outside and dried them at the saloon fire and put them in Lillie's and Fannie's bunks to make them think some of the others had done it.

Lillie and Fannie went and sat on the bridge and I came up on deck too, and it was cold so the 2nd. Mate fixed an old sail up to shelter us, but the wind got our legs, and he saw Fannie fixing her dress so as to keep warm and came along and said "your feet are getting cold A?" and went and got another sail and fixed it up to shelter our legs, good man and we had a fine warm seat. I got some biscuits and Lillie and Fannie fought for biscuits and "Nimble" was at the wheel grinning like old boots. Then we went ashore on the Antipodes, and we landed and saw heaps of penguins and a goat and a kid that hopped over the rocks at the rate of knots it was so pretty, pale creamy colour. We landed the heffer more dead than alive and had to drag her up the hill, they had an awful job to haul her up the hill, she was so weak she could hardly stand, and they left the poor little cow on the first broard safe place where there was plenty of coarse grass. Captain and Moffet went off to-gether, the carpenter went down to look at the depot and when he was coming up the hill again Fannie and I sang out to him " *I say* what and where and that and that and that did you *did you Carpenter*?" we said the "I say" plain so he could hear and the "did you? Carpenter did You?" and said the rest so he could not catch what we said and he stopped on the other side to try and hear what we said and we only laughed at him, and said "*no but Carpenter*, bumble bumble bumble something or other *did you? Carpenter did you*?" and he said "I'm but a wee thing, dull o' hearin!" and laughed and went on out of sight. We 3 kept on falling down every two minutes, it was awful stuff to get through all the tussocks were like nigger heads and deep gutters in between. The only way we found them out was by falling into them, and it wasn't easy to get out again. We saw we saw the cattle, a red and a white, and a dead sheep over by some underground holes in a little gulley.

We ran after heaps of parakeats plain green and I did fall down heaps of times and had my hand on some heaps of times and threw my ulster over some and got none. We had fine fun after a lot of parakeats and some such beauties bigger than the ordinary ones, and a most lovely green we nearly caught a lot they were so tame, and I fell head first between two nigger heads and got stuck by the shoulders and Lillie had to pull me out by the legs. I caught a snipe and let it go again and we saw Sea hawks and had fine times up there.

We told Pat where to go for parakeats, and he ran like old boots, to find them, and Fannie told "Nimble" to throw his cap at a parakeat, and he did and it got away and the 2nd. Mate sat down and talked to us about Toi Tois. Captain hove into view over the cliff carrying a heavy fat lamb, he was just about done fore, and when he saw the 2nd. Mate sitting down talking to us he was wild and half dead with heat and said "why don't you go and haul the cow up,? sitting there idle and me carrying this lamb" The 2nd. Mate went down the hill faster than I could say, and "Nimble" heard him, and took the hint and went down in a few jumps. Lillie carried the lamb for Captain down to the rocks and it was jolly heavy, and when "Nimble" went to carry it to the boat Lillie said "it's pretty heavy" he said "oh it taint so very heavy" and hoisted it onto his shoulder and strutted off like the giant in the 7 leagued boots. We put off in the dingy and left "Alabastor" and "Marryeanus" and we saw the goat and the lovely little white kid it flew over the rocks like a lamplighter.

"I say!! what about the birds?" – don't critiscise please.

119

After parakeets on the Antipodes

Friday October 31st 1890.

After parakeets on the Antipodes

We brought off about 50 penguins and when we got on board the dingy went off with the 2nd. Mate and a lot of others to get the other two and on round to another penguin rookery and the boat harbor. They came back after T and got dozens of birds and eggs by the hundred, and we left about 7 from the Antipodes for the Bounties after T and I am sorry for that I can tell you.

Its all Moffet's fault, he is in such a darned hurry to get within hail of a butcher's shop and newspaper. There are 2 live Albertrosses on board besides all the penguins fenced in aft and a Sea hawk and our 2 sea lions, and next after T we practise and "Alabastor" and "Moondyne" play draughts and we stayed up till 11 "Alabastor" nearly fainted when he looked at the time and found how late we were up, and we turned in at 12 I did, and slept sound all night.

Saturday
1st November 1890

Here we are at daylight in sight of the Bounties, a lovely fine warm sunny morning to begin with, so we got up early, made a good start so far, and we got there after breakfast, and the penguins were just in thousands all over the rocks.

We saw a white "Nellie" flying about and heaps of Ice birds, and a fine lovely morning and we went ashore after breakfast 16 of us in the big boat. We went to the largest of the 16 Islands, it was almost too rough to land, the "Hinemoa" was rolling like fury, and we didn't want Captain to look back at her or he would not want to land. We told Moffet there was a white Nellie to try and coax him to stop, great owl he wanted to go right on and not land. We went into the gulch to land where there are fine natural steps up the cliff when you get ashore but it is jolly hard to get there, it is a most frantic rough place to land and the waves rising and falling from 20 to 25 feet all the time.

At first Captain said no one was to land, then only the Carpenter and Moffet to go, then made some of the hands get out and haul up some of the timber for building a depot but it was too rough to do anything today. Captain thought we aughtn't to land (hang it!!) we *were* wild – and he told one of the hands Nelson to rest one end of the timber on a rock above his shoulder, and because he happened to look down Captain said "just look at him looking at his knees for his shoulder". Every one landed but us, Captain went ashore and left us with two hands, and the 2nd. Mate in the boat. We *did look black* and growled away to ourselves, we were *cross*. The 2nd. Mate said he was sure we could land and seemed quite sorry for us to be left. He gave Lillie an Ice birds egg. As soon as Captain came back he let us go ashore, no wonder, our faces must have said a good deal. We got out of the boat fine, "Merryeanus" stood on the rocks and gave us a hand and every time she would rise on a wave close to the rocks her bows were full of kelp and it kept slipping out over the bows as she came up, when she was up we made a jump and were ashore in two shakes. We went up the rocks up kind of steps, the birds were there in 100's and the Molly hawks were sitting and the Ice birds and penguins.

121

On top of the Bounty Islands.

We were *so glad* to get ashore, when we got up to the birds first thing Fannie did was to haul a Molly hawk off its nest by the tail, I gave one a lift out over the rocks by the two wings and the poor beggar fell down plump on the rocks, I was so sorry for it. Someone said they could not fly when they were sitting and I wanted to try if they could. I kept on poking at them on purpose to hear them sing out the birds were just in thousands all around about and flying about above all the Islands in millions, the air was thick with them, the row they made was enough to deafen you, there were Sea hawks, Molly hawks, Ice birds, penguins and Nellies and heaps of other kinds. We caught some Ice birds and let them go again, Fannie hung on to hers till we went to get down and had to let them go to get down herself. We only stayed about 5 minutes on top when we had to go back "Moondyne" and Moffet went away over. Coming down all those in the boat must have had a fine view of our legs.

We got into the boat middling well, and came back on board, and Lillie's scarf went away out to sea ever so far and the boat had to go for it. Then another lot went ashore and brought back about a ton of different eggs but they nearly all had chickens in them. We brought off no end of eggs too and some penguins and Molly hawks and Ice birds, they had to throw the buckets of eggs into the boat when we were getting in and half got smashed and the boat was in such a mess.

Captain wanted a bit of string on the bridge, he sent "Gilpin" to get it and he didn't turn up so he sent Arthur and he could not find it so he sent two more and they were away on the hunt, Martin was at the wheel and he said to him *Martin you make the fifth man* and sent him off too. We went along to the galley and Fannie asked the cook for some plums and said it was her birthday, the plums were all used, so she asked for a tart and at last the cook gave her half of one, and Fannie said "he's going to give us *all* this" the cook said *"No he's not"*. We ran away and ate it and Fannie went back to thank him for it and he gave her the rest of it then we came into our cabin and ate it, it was good too, but hot just out of the oven.

We left the Islands after dinner and that was the last we saw of the Bounties and after dinner "Moondyne" gave Fannie 2 tarts. We sat on deck for a bit till it began to blow hard and got too cold, the spray was coming over fore and aft, so we came down and stood by the glass and Fannie told Charlie to tie up "Nimbles" things in the fidley. He said he would but got sick before he had time, it was rough and blowing hard. We watched "Merryeanus" taking down the looking glass in the end cabin, Fannie took his cap and put it out in the wet, he came to pay her out and Fannie made out she was sick so he let her go again. After T "Alabastor" and I played draughts Lillie and Fannie were standing there again looking at Pantry and Pat carrying along coal to the galley, Pantry is a fright he had on a bun, and a long tailed coat, and gumboots and all together looked extremely handsom. (Last night "Alabastor" Lillie and Fannie went along to the galley and looked at him and Arthur cooking and eating penguin eggs – we did laugh at them. Arthur was shovelling his up with a spoon with a handle about a mile long.)

The seas are coming over right and left tonight, Nelson got half drowned near the fidley with a big sea, just as he had taken off his coat too. Pat and Fannie had a barney over "Nimble". Pat asked if old Blair was the one? and Fannie said yes. Pat was a mean old beggar and wouldn't tell "Nimbles" name. It is jolly cold and rough tonight, Pat said "Nimbles" name was *"All-dust"*. Arthur is trying to blow bad Molly hawks eggs and making more noise than his head is worth, we turn in early and slept.

Sunday
2nd November 1890

I dreampt of a picture and woke and we were out at sea on our way to Port Chalmers and we had a head wind and it was rough, and it is a fine morning, but cold, and away we go back worse luck.

We had some of the lamb for dinner and T and he was good and appricot tart for dinner too. We saw a penguin making tracks for home (south) jumping through the water at the rate of knots. Pat's wrinkle forrard mate used to be on the "Ocean Mail" she got wrecked on the Chathams going home from Wellington. "Moondyne" told us how all the waiters on a steamer he was on, some big boat, were stopped smoking on deck, so they all chewed tobacco at tea and spit on the mat every time they passed the Captns. chair, he soon let them smoke on deck again. Fannie put something in Pantry's boots she thought they were "Nimbles" and "Gilpin" said he would tell the first police man he met, and he gave us some eggs. Pat found out "Nimbles" name, and it is *"Alexandia George Petersen"* so he says, and he said it was *Axel*, who knows what it is? After dinner Lillie and I sat on the settee for a bit and it was cold, and the 2nd. Mate is very friendly, and is going to show me how to make a star knot, I wanted him to show me then, but he said "after 4 o'clock A!", "Merryeanus" showed us a model he had started of a ship. "Moondyne" gave us 3 tarts after dinner, and we ate them.

We waited down between the doors and the fidley and the 2nd Mate showed me how to make a star knot, I was trying all kinds of knots all day. Captain told us about the Maori he said good morning to, and the Maori said "no fear no good morning to you" because he had hammered him in a boat one time for cheeking the Native Minister, and Captain pulled the plug out of it to scare him. He told us of another Maori who tried to come into the cabin when he was tite and the Governor was there, and Captain stopped him, and he fell on deck in a pool of water and lay there and wouldn't get up till the Govenor came and saw where Captain had put him. His cloths soaked up most of the water and Captain got a broom and swept the rest of it away the Maori told the Govenor Captain had kicked his legs from under him when he least expected it, what an old crammer.

Every time the "Hinemoa" rolled Fannie clacked the dish covers together to tease "Gilpin" and he popped his head out of his door and said "you'll be smashing all the dishes in the ship next Miss Richardson" and was wild too, The 2nd. Mate has learnt all ready *aye* it must be the situation if not what can it be? When Lillie and Fannie were eating ham and I had some too, "Marryeanus" was in there, we always go for the ham and pickles when we can. The other day "Alabastor" called out to "Moondyne" that his can was running over he said it was too full, and "Moondyne" said "what" and he said "the sink pot is running over" We went up to bunk and had fine fun acting in our cabin in our garments we tied stockings round our waists to look better and we sung *"when the ship is trim and ready and the jolly days are done"* to a rum tune and "why did he die? because he did!" and we danced about in front of our big glass all the time and roared laughing. Fannie made "Presto" forwards and "Lento" going backwards and O! we did laugh, its a wonder we didn't wake all hands and the cook, then we turned in and soon we were asleep all in a row in our bunks.

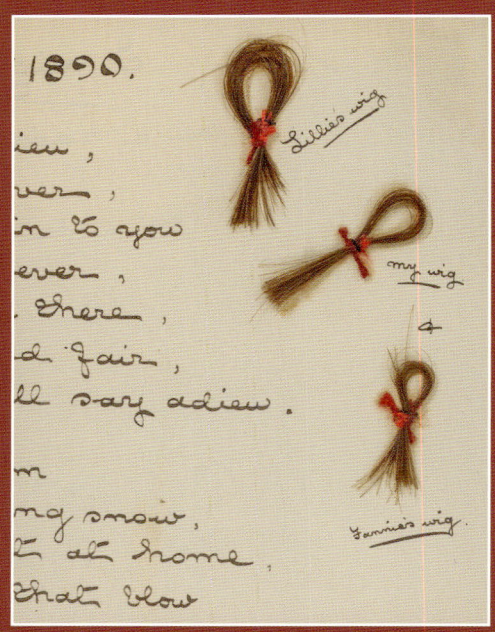

1890.

...ieu ,
...ver ;
...in to you
...ever ,
...there ,
...d fair ,
...ll say adieu .

...m
...ng snow ,
...t at home ,
...that blow

Lillie's wig

my wig

4

Fannie's wig .

TRUE

1891.

(We dress in black lining,
to save washing dresses.)

Monday
3rd November 1890

I deampt and woke up and still blowing hard and a ship on the port bow. Cold and cloudy today, "Alabastor" was more humbug than enough, we brushed our ulsters, and sighted land about eight.

We exchanged eggs with "Alabastor" and he gave us two sea eggs big ones from Jacksons bay, and I gave him my sea lions skulls big and little, after breakfast, I write and here I am at it and we are in sight of land and will be in in about an hour to Port Chalmers and all yesterday we were out at sea on the way from the Bounties, and we will soon be in. I am sorry. Saw the ship standing away out, Lillie got "Alabastors" plants out for "Merryeanus" and he took her snufpoke (last night when Lillie and Fannie first went into the pantry to eat ham). In came "Alabastor" to cut up tobacco, then he went out again and "Merryeanus" came in and we gave him some ham on biscuit, he went for Fannie and she said she was sick, and her hand was hurt, and heaps of things but no go, so in dispair she said "Oh! for goodness sake kiss me and be done with it" and they nearly sat in the rubbish bucket in the corner. "Merryeanus" made a dive for me when I was sitting very comfortable in the corner of the saloon, and I said *in a most miserable voice* "Ah! no Carpenter, Iv'e got such a head ache" (?) so out of pity he left me –

A schooner came in close behind us sailing very fast, and saw the barque "Kingdom of Sweden" anchored out and we saw the "Ranee" sunk in the channel near the quarentine station, she caught fire and had to be scuttled. We got into Port Chalmers at mid day and we got to the wharf about 12. After, we went ashore and telegraphed to Ma and then went up to Miss Sinclair at the school and found her and went on board again and she came down to see the sea lions.

It came on to rain heavy and a lot of people came and looked at the sea lions and some of them called them sea elephants, and Fannie said *"they are Sea lions and we helped catch them"* and fair fat Bobbie that was on looking at them said "O!" and "nonsense!" and I told him there was a *rum spider* aft, and a lot of birds, and off he went to look for them, and they all strung after him I hope he finds the spider anyway. Pat laughed, because I said I wished some of the birds would go for them.

"Three old maids are we —
"Aye youre no   Mun mun a aye   Aye but still
as slim as   widna hae thought   we may tak
yaw use'd."   we'd get sa awfa fat."   a sma step:"

Miss Sinclair had a look at the sea lions and birds and told us she had a scrumptious tea for us, and we went with Miss Sinclair for our scrumptious tea (of dirt) but the stew had a rum taste it had some kind of seeds in it and bits of black, and the marmalade jar hadn't been washed out since the last time we were there. After tea went and sat up in the garden on a seat by the tree-mingnonette, and said soon these days would be gone and we would think of them. It was nice sitting there, then we went in and yarned over the trip, and tried our music Miss Sinclair gave us (good old soul) she gave us each a book of it, we played on her violin, and Fannie tried to make a bargin with her for her old violin, Miss Sinclair's has a lovely tone, and Fannie offered to give her – her own violin, 2 pounds, a dressed up photo, and a packet of hair pins, for it but Miss Sinclair didn't see it. We had supper, we had some of the kerosene cocoa, then made tracks for the "Hinemoa".

Miss S came part of the way, and Captain came to meet us, we met him half down the hill, we stopped for a few minutes and listened to the band playing, Miss Sinclair left us at the Town hall, Old Jenny gave us a fine bunch of wallflowers, before we left, we gave some to Captain, and sent some aft, before we went up to Miss Sinclair's we said good bye to "Alabastor" who took ages to dress and went off in a higious bun – I hate them – in stead of his cap he used to wear on board. I gave "Moondyne" 6 jolly good dumps with a cushion in "Alabastors" cabin. The "Matatua" is in and the "Duke of Buckingham" and barque "Langstone" all painted up looking spiff. Got back on board and turned in at 10. I hate getting so near the end of the trip–

129

Tuesday
4th November 1890

I dreampt of "Moondyne" and woke with Arthur banging at our door, enough to rouse the dead. He might well bang to wake me, he woke us early, we told him to, and Captain called out from his cabin and asked what he was making all that row about? and Arthur said "they asked me to call them early sir".

At 8 I wasn't half dressed, and the train went at a quarter past. I shovelled on my things and Fannie and I ran down and gobbled some breakfast wholesale, there was liver and bacon, and some lovely tea-cake. Lillie wouldn't come for any she hadn't time and we quadded down our breakfast mine stuck half way down I swallowed it in such a hurry. I was eating some T-cake and the bell rang, we all ran, I couldn't bear to leave my T-cake so I put a whole bit of T-cake in to my mouth as I ran off and it stuck there half way down all day.

We did run to catch the train, it was raining like old boots, the Mate and "Nimble" stared at us as we ran for the train. It began to move before we were off the wharf, we thought we couldn't catch it, and stopped till someone called out (to run on we'd get it) and we ran on again and got it and just got on. I was between Lillie and Fannie and didnt know wether to catch up to Fannie or wait for Lillie, if I caught up to Fannie we couldn't go on without Lillie, and if I stopped 4 Lillie we'd be too late, I kept looking at the engine driver as much as to say "O! can't you wait for 3 poor beggars running their hardest". I thought he'd take pity on us and so he did because he slacked in a bit for us, and some ass called out "O you'll never catch it" that's why we stopped running but we just got on.

We try to be funny

Fannie and I jumped onto a smoking carrage, the train was going all the time and Lillie was so limp she ran and put one knee on the step of the last carrage and stuck there for a minute till she got enough breath to get up. A boy said "let me help you" and took her gamp till she got up, she was just off the step in time for the tunnel. First little station we got to Fannie and I got off the smoking carrage and went to Lillie, there was a very nice cock eyed guard and he got us a pass of some kind in Dunedin, it was jolly cold and wet, we got up to Dunedin and went to Post office, no letters, so got the tram and went out to Mrs Kydd. A man (Deveral's skeleton) got into the tram, and we 3 thought it was him and Lillie said to him "Are you Mr Deveral?" and he gave her awfull eyes and shook his head, and Lillie said "O, I beg your pardon I thought you were".

We took Mrs Kydd a lot of plants from the Islands, and found Mr Kydd at home and Nellie and Jessie. Lillie gave Mrs Kydd the plants and labelled them for her, they were all so glad to see us. We had a good time of it there, and got heaps of flowers, and green goosegogs, we came to dinner and had a grand dinner, and such a swig of milk that *washed down my tea-cake* ("*thank 'eaven*") Lillie collared no end of flowers, we took some green goosberrys back on board. We left to come back at a quarter 2 2. Jessie came down to the tram with us and Nellie came in it as far as her dressmaking place.

The people all stared at us from the tram to the train, and Lillie lost her lovely rose Nellie gave her at the post office, we came down by the half past 2 train, and saw "Merryeanus" and Charlie carrying a box on the platform. We got on board and I gave "Moondyne" some green goos gogs and a bunch of flowers, we devided the flowers, and a bunch to "Gilpin" and "Merryeanus" and some 4 aft, we were jolly wild to see she-males on board, and we have two passengers hang them, owls! and with a darned little black dog that kept on going into our cabin, fleay little fright. The birds and sea lions are all gone, and we are just off and off we just went before tea, we went and looked at Governor's grey horse forrard, and I platted its mane and "Milk-and-water" came past and asked me to do his hair the same way, I said "it's too short, *clack clack clack you've 'ad your 'air cut*". Fannie gave the Mate two sour green goosberrys, and he said "thanks" and she gave some to "Merryeanus" and "Moondyne", we got a telegram from Ma ("*all well*").

Mr and Mrs Blackwood are our passengers names, and at T Mr Blackwood said "Mrs Blackwood had a head ache and wasn't coming to T, she didn't like the motion" she was sick I'll bet. After T we practised and I copied the "Olgar Waltz", after tea, Lillie left the bathroom port open and a big wave came and filled it and came into our cabin too. "Gilpin" was wild and said "we would sink the ship one of these days" and he and "Moondyne" and Arthur all ran to mop up. Lillie gave "Merryeanus" a bunch of flowers, and Captain came and saw him with them and glared. It was fine most of the day poor old Captain got a big wave over him this evening, and got doused through. Fannie gave Arthur a bit of "Time" for Pat and he tore a birthday card off the wall by his bunk and sent it along to Fannie, and she sent "Nimble" a pansy as a buttonhole to wear in Lyttelton, and he said "he would dream on it". He dodged her in the fidley and wouldn't answer to the name of Petersen, Arthur said "oh we always call him Alf".

We start fading away

Fannie sent a "Pink" to "Merryeanus" and he said "he would keep it as a **momento**". We send Arthur all our messages. In the evening "Moondyne" told us of the Suez canal being blocked, and how hundreds of steamers were all stuck there and how they danced all night, and all his addresses. I showed him all the addresses in my little notebook and he told us about the diferent places, Slopers island and all the rest of it, and 7 sisters road, and he comes from Deal in Kent. "Moondyne" was good he gave us a jug of milk and we had it in the pantry, and some cake he gave us for supper. Before we got the milk Fannie said "she was awfully thirsty and asked what he used the jugs for? – did he ever put milk in them?" He was sensible enough to take the hint and gave us a jug full to our own cheek and you bet it disappeared in a very short time. We turned in at 12 and slept our way to Lyttelton, and a fine night.

Wednesday
5th November 1890

Woke I up and found ourselves close to land and the "Brunner" and an American ship and I am sad at heart we will soon be in. We passed a ship in the night heading south, and we passed the Yank, full rigged, about breakfast time making in to Lyttelton, as well as us.

It came on to rain very heavy when we were coming up the harbour and kept up till dinner time and we got to Lyttelton at 11, and came along side and left the wharf and moved further to the baths and made fast there just before dinner.

First thing, a boy offered me a paper, and I said "I would have it without the penny but otherwise it was too expensive" the boy looked at me and went on. Mrs Blackwood is too sick to show up, so much the better for us, and the first thing Fannie saw "Nimble" she said "well what did you dream?"– he didn't dream anything. I was down at the music looking at what Miss Sinclair put in my book. It was raining no more.

Lillie and Fannie watched the "Oger" shovelling down coal, and I came up and stood there out by the doors by the fidley. The "Oger" got some buckets of water to wash down when he had finished, and Fannie got a broom and broomed up the deck and Pat tipped up a bucket Fannie had and wet her feet and shoes and splattered her. Fannie told him "he was a stupid old devil" and she got the "Oger to get her some more water in a bucket, she tipped out some and went and poured the rest down the fidley on top of Pat's head she knew she was safe when he was so far down. He said he would pay her out, and he told Fannie "she was a regular old salt" because she knew the rigs of vessels, and before dinner we went to the galley, and Fannie asked the cook for something good as it was her birthday, (she had many birthdays at the galley door). Fannie plagued his life as usual, poor old beggar he was so hot, we were sorry for him. Fannie kept on asking, and at last he took up a knife and said "*dam it*" and cut off a bit of tart or jam roll and gave it to Fannie in a pot lid and said "*I would like to call her a little devil*". We did laugh and Fannie praised him and said he was good and thanked him for the tart, she said "thanks for the tart my word you're awfully good in fact the best on the whole ship as far as being agreeable goes". He thought she wanted something more, because she kept on praising him, we came into our cabin and ate the tart, it was just red hot *but very good.*

Then we started teasing "Merryeanus", and we kept on to him "down there the other day (all mumbeldy) *did you, Carpenter, did you*?" and he said "no I did not yet but I will and serve you right too" and I said "bumble bumble something the other day, will you! Carpenter, will you?" and he said "yes I will before the trip is done" and I said "if you don't, I will" and he said "that's right, then I'll think it a regular love affair and die happy" and we did laugh I can tell you,

"To meet, to know, to love and be apart,
Is the fate of many a heart."

I wrote this b4 dinner when we first went alongside we went under the ship "Lurline's" stern, but of course didn't stay ten minutes then went over to the wharf next the baths where no ships are. Two apprentices were up aloft and came down and stood under the foksle and looked over the edge, and it was raining hard too, the ship "Waipa", the brigantine "Jessie" and the 4 master "Strathgryfe" 2190 tons, and the barque "Onyx" are all in. We got a fine long letter from Ma, 6 pages and a half, the other day we sneaked 2 tins of fish out of the pantry and we ate our tins of *salmon* and *NZ mullet*. We had the tin opener and we got 3 spoons and one plate, and Lillie emptied the whole vinegar bottle in on top of the lot, out of the cruet in the saloon. I told Lillie not to empty it all out or "Moondyne" would know, but she did, and we went in our cabin and ate the whole lot in no time, and "Moondyne" heard us laughing, and clacking our plates, he was in the next cabin. We put the tins out the port hole, and we nearly threw the tins on "Ogers" head and "Nimble", they were painting over the side.

Fannie showed "Nimble" her dressed up photo out our port, and he asked her "how she got a moustache?" and said "it was well taken" and we could hardly waddle, after our feast and weren't a scrap hungry for tea. "Moondyne" and Arthur were on the wharf today shaking the runners. We were on the bridge and saw a girl coming down the wharf, and I asked "Merryeanus" "if it was his sweetheart" he said "yes, and yon is yours carrying the boots up the wharf". The one carrying the boots was a most larrikin looking boy in shoes with yellow socks, *and breeches too short*, and *two* silver rings on *one* finger, and smoking a sigerette so I asked the carpenter "if it was only sixpence to get his boot mended?" he said "my word I will give it to you" and I said "Ah no surely not when I'm your best friend" he said "O, then I'll leave ye alone" and I said "oh you're a good old friend after all".

We can't settle to anything today and feel very savage we are so near the end of our trip and a jolly good one its been too in spite of the bad weather, and after T we went in to the cemetry and looked at it. We didn't see a single nice tomb-stone, but some lovely beautiful flowers, some red roses with a most heavenly scent, we were nearly tempted to pick them there was some lovely mingnonette too with a lovely scent, and Lillie said "no one could blame a middie for ever picking one, when they see so few". We got some grass on the hill for the sheep, and went back at dusk. We found the English Church in Winchester St, we had a fine stroll round, and there was a most lovely sunset, and it lighted up all the hill tops round.

The whole afternoon was fine, and we came on board and fed the poor old sheep, and it is a regular chum of the grey horse all ready and stands underneath it for safety, the poor old horse looked on with a jealous eye when it saw the sheep eating the grass so we gave it a wee bit too.

Mr. Blackwood and his wife got moved over to our side of the ship today, next to *my* cabin too, just so we can't have any fun going to bed. He did nothing but talk of H.M.S. Nilson all the time, his little pug nosed dog is called Nero, and is a Japaneese, it was running up and down the bridge whining its heart out because it couldn't get onto the wharf to its boss. I had a game of draughts with "Moondyne" and Lillie and Fannie were walking up and down in the electric light for a long time, it was such a beautiful evening and so warm. "Merryeanus" said he had Fannie's photo and showed us an old Judge cigarette photo, that was very like her.

The Yank we passed out at sea this morning came in, the "Coptic" came in too at 10, and "Moondyne" wanted us to go and have a look at her, but Lillie would not, and he went over to her, and we went out by the fidley and ran the "Coptic" down. Fannie called her a "prig" and Lillie called her a "cad" and I a "snob", and I said "I would rather one day on the "Hinemoa" than 20 on her, and if you put your foot past the first class part your toe is chopped off with a tommy hawk". Freeberg was watchman, and went slouching over to have a look too, and Lillie said "I don't blame him, if I was watchman I'd do the same, and go uptown and sit in a hotel half the night, instead of shivering and shaking on the foksle all the time" and we went down and ate biscuits and butter, in the pantry. "Moondyne" showed us last night the American and French way of toasting, in the pantry, and Lillie called him "an old masher" because he used scent, and we turned in about 11 *very dumpy*, and slept all night.

137

Homeward Bound

Thursday
6th November 1890

I dreampt, and woke up, and got up early, its fine but cloudy and first thing after breakfast we moved across under the cranes and away from the "Coptic", and they started loading before we were near the wharf and tried to kill "Nimble" by making him stand under the heavy iron things getting loaded on - and I am writing, and we are sad at heart, and, and, I will stop now--

We stood on deck and critasized everybody who came near, and at 10 we went for a pull and got a boat painted blue and called "Minnie", a nice boat with **lead oars,** and we had a real good pull, round outside the breakwater, round by the "Leading Wind" and "Waipa" and someone on a stage under the ships counter stared most awfully and even leant out to look. Then we went outside, and Fannie was sitting in the bows, and the driver on the engine called out "why didn't she pull instead of leaning back taking it easy in the bows?" we only looked at him and went on and we went inside again and round all the ships and "Coptic". We came in and paid our old man, and told him his oars were jolly heavy, and the old boatman said "we could pull as well as he could". After dinner Lillie and I went ashore, and Fannie stopped on board and helped the "Oger" varnish all the bright-work (to the astonishment of all passers by) she asked Captain could she? and he said she could. Fannie hated varnishing with the "Oger", and told him to stop or she wouldn't go on, and cheeked and scolded him right and left one minute but next yarned friendly whenever she wanted to ask him anything. He knows Toi Tois well, old brute. Captain and Lillie and Fannie saw some tight Yankee sailors coming down the wharf.

Sketches of The Chatham, Antipodes and Snares Islands

Away went Lillie and I shopping (?) the dark in the dark (Lillie) and the light in the light (me) (dresses). We went into nearly every shop in the place, and Lillie got gloves (to try and come home decent) and I told the man "the gloves were long enough for stockings". Lillie sent a telegram to Ma, and she only had *3 pence* left so got it in conversations. We did have fun shopping, and we wanted something for "Moondyne", and "Merryeanus", and we went back for more cash, and I went aboard and got it. We went back and got a little book arrangement for "Moondyne", and "Merryeanus" with "Won't you?" on it, and we got some sugar men and things, and a lollie face for "Moondyne", and a pink breechied little fright for "Merryeanus", and one for "Nimble", and a yellow fool for Pat. Then we went into a shop and got a coccoanut, just so we could ask for a rose, and I asked the man for a rose and he said "you may 'ave one if you can get it out". The bunch of flowers was tied up tight with string, and I got two, a cream, and a pink one, both buds, he glared but didn't say anything, because I asked for 1 and took 2, I suppose. We went a good way round by the baths, and along to the house where the butterfly was in the garden, caught in a spider web, and Lillie went and took it out (on our way back from the Chatham Islands).

We saw some lovely roses, and heaps of other good flowers, so Lillie went into the "butterfly house" and asked for a drink of water (*and got sent to the pump*!! –) and praised the old woman's flowers up to the nineties, and the old woman helped praise them, but at the same time she wouldn't take the hint and give Lillie one and she came away without any. I stood at the gate all the time grinning, so we left her, and went to another house with such lovely cream roses climbing all over the side, so Lillie went there for another drink of water, and praised the roses, and a great lanky boy gave Lillie a glass *and pointed to the tank* "they are mighty rude in Lyttelton" said Lillie. The boy would not take the hint, and he was too jolly grumpy to ask for flowers, so we gave it up as a bad job. I was holding her rose bud at the gate (mine was the pink) and in trying to fix it in again she knocked its head off. I told her it served her right for being so greedy, she pinned it on, so we went back on board and delivered our goods, and sent the lollies to all the different ones and had fine fun.

"Nimble" went past with his tea, and Fannie said "is that for me?" and he said "yes, oh yes but there's nothing here" and we left just after T, at a quarter to 7. Just as we were starting, we saw a drunk man going to the "Leading Wind". He was a tite sailor, a very red yank, he went past after nearly walking over the edge into the sea more than once, and he kept on talking to the hands and got on board his ship, and as we steamed past he popped up and down behind the bullwarks forrard and said "good bye my love" and flourished his arms and kissed hands to everybody, and kept singing out "goodbye me love, goodbye".

We passed the "Linder Weber" going down the harbour, waiting for a fair wind, and passed "Annie Wilson" very nearly out. "Nimble" was at the wheel, and Lillie and Fannie kept trying to focus their eyes to see him in the dusk, then they came down and we plagued "Moondyne" in the end cabin. He was making a bunk, and we put sheets over his head, and wound him up in them, and we ran away with everything, and Arthur grabbed the end of the blanket and tried to haul it from us into the saloon, Fannie took his cap. Lillie and Fannie were up talking to "Merryeanus", then we stood by the fidley in the little alleyway, and "Merryeanus" showed us the limpet shell from Sunday Island, and Lillie asked the 2nd. Mate the long words in maori, and he offered to be pilot on our "schooner" if we gave them good food. Fannie had on "Moondyne's" coat all evening. "Nilson" turned in early, we went below and "Moondyne" took my rose so I kept putting blotting paper down his neck. I picked up my pen and went in the pantry and Lillie and Fannie ate all the raddishes for supper. They found them in the pantry in a bucket. "Moondyne" gave us a jug of milk, and we stayed up till 12, it was a fine evening and we turned in and slept I did–at first I could not sleep at all, and we were sad and nearly howling because the trip is just ended–

Lillie pushed the door shut and told Fannie and I a yarn. I sat on the brass between their cabin and mine and Fannie was in bunk and soon we were fast asleep all in a row.

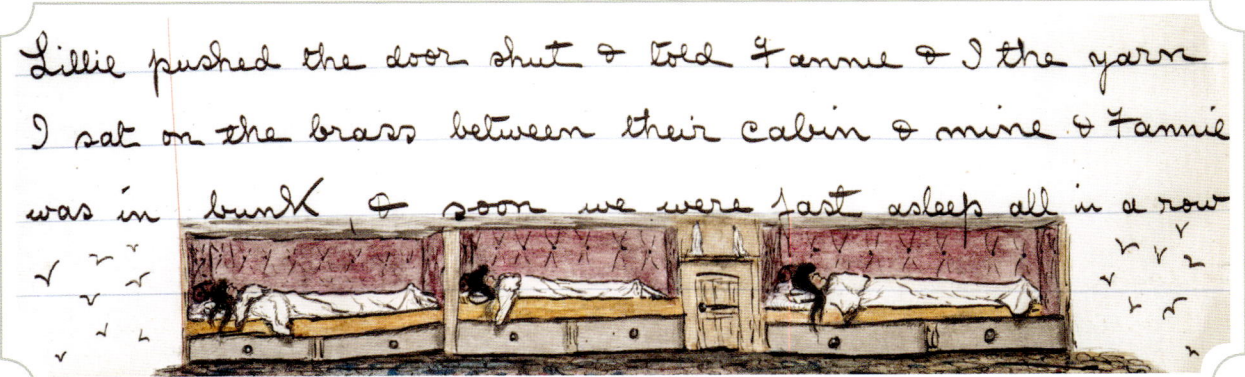

Soon we were fast asleep all in a row.

Friday
7th November 1890

We got up very early, and saw the "Wairarapa" and we packed up our things, and I'll never forget these days – "Moondyne" came to call us and we made out to be crying. Lillie and Fannie went on deck first and a most lovely fresh breeze on deck.

We have a regular list to port, with the timber on the bridge, and we passed a ship in the night bound north, a steamer. Fannie cheeked Pat and the "Oger" and she asked Pat "where the Carpenter was?" he said "he's not up yet he's sleepy poor fellow after being kept up so late last night". Fannie said "I didn't keep him up" he said "no, but Lillie did" so Lillie said "it wasn't me only, Ethel was there too" he said "Oh no she wasn't she had better fish to fry, she was down below" and Fannie asked him "who would be sorry when we were gone?" he said the Carpenter would, and Petersen, and one of the stewards, Marsh". The "Oger" and "Nimble" were washing the fidley and a wave came over and soaked "Nimble", and the "Oger" escaped – *what a pity* – Fannie said to Pat "what a pity it wasn't you who got wet" and he told "Nimble" "Fannie said she wished he had got drowned" mean old beggar.

Fannie teased the poor cook, till he gave us each a wee tart, she told the cook "it was truly her birthday today she could shake hands on it". The cook said "oh no you have cried wolf too often". Fannie said "aren't you going to give me anything for the last day?" Then he said he would give us 3 wee marmalade tarts if we came along to the galley, so Lillie went and got them, and Fannie gave hers to "Nimble" and he said "thonks" and ate it straight away. Fannie went to get another, and the cook wouldn't let her, and upset the whole dish of them on the wet galley floor trying to take it from her. – *He stamped* and said "*dam the thing*" and Fannie ran for bare life, and when the cook came along a few minutes after, Fannie said "thanks for the tarts Cook, but I am awfully sorry the dish upset" he said "oh you're a little rogue, had you been a boy you would have many a thrashing this trip" and Fannie said "but you shouldn't swear, you said *dam*" and he said "why I was only blessing the dish". He went and looked into the fidley, and Fannie said "what are you looking at in there?" He said "I was thinking of 'ome girl, I don't get much of it." then he said "he wished we were coming North, as it made the old man better tempered to have someone with him."

This is the last morning and Lillie is writing sitting on the stairs, the 2nd. Mate is on watch, and I kept on saying "did you?" to "Merryeanus". Fannie was giving "Nimble' lollies, and it is a truly lovely day, and a fine breeze, and we can see the heads and it is blowing a bit now. Abreast of Cape Campbell it came on to blow hard, the "Wairarapa" was in company with us there, "Nimble" was at the wheel, and we 3 went and stood at the foot of the stairs and made out we were howling, and "Nimble" laughed so much he had to put his head behind the mast. The 2nd. Mate wondered what was up and backed over to the wheel and looked down to see, and only saw us standing not doing anything. In the straits we passed the ship "Auckland" and barque "Brussels" coming up the harbour it was blowing great guns, and spray coming over in all directions. We were quite wild having to come back, the man-o-war "Curiso" is anchored out in the harbour, and a barque the "Star of the East" and the ship "Orari" is at the Railway wharf and the "Alcoyne", and the New Zealand shipping Co's baque "Rakia" is at the main wharf. Par and the boys came down to meet us. King is 7 miles high, and Harry ordering us right and left to come home at once and get dinner, we were down right glad to see all their dear faces once more–

144

The return of the Hinemoa

ye'll just hae to excuse our backs noo!!

When we were coming across the straits the little angora goat had to be put down below as it was getting drowned, it was jolly rough too. We went down to the pantry and said goodbye to Arthur, and he dried his hand and said "Oh! I wish you were coming North with us" and we said goodbye to "Gilpin" and "Moondyne" and the Cook and "Pantry", and said goodbye to all the others and "Nimble" who made out to be howling. We met Annie Fairchild just as we were going off, and we went down the wharf and said goodbye to the 2nd. Mate. He was on the wharf by the "Hinemoa's" stern, and we went and I *was* sorry, Kennerly wouldn't take all our boxes in his precious old cab, disagreeable old hound, he didn't fancy carrying *hams*, and plants in boxes "Merryeanus" had made.

We drove home in fine style, and found Ma all alive O! and a *jolly good* dinner which we ate *every bit* of although we had just had dinner on the "Hinemoa" – and a goosberry and rubarb tart and it was very good. Ma had flowers everywhere for us and in our old room, and they were *so* lovely, and the garden is so beautiful, simply beautiful, and poor little "Image" was so glad to see me she hopped all round among us, she was almost more over joyed than all, dear little "Imey" – After dinner we undid all our rattle-traps, and left them all over our room, it was a regular sight, and about 5 we went back down to the "Hinemoa" to find my gamp, that I left in my cabin, and I got it, and we saw Martin and he said "we aught to come North" we saw "Merryeanus" and he seemed quite doudy, and Lillie got her moss from "Moondyne" and we came away very dumpy. We were doudy, and after T we practised and had supper and a fine one it was. We had cakes and ginger ale (that I hate) all for the return of we 3, then we gabbled away and all the rest of it, till all hours of the night.

"We've just come home from the sea today
And browned and bronzed are we,
For many's the day we've been away
In the "Hinemoa" over the sea"

We turned in after having a scrumptious bath about 12 all amongst the rubbish in our room, and slept once more in our old beds, with my picture of the "Hinemoa" swinging above us, and Fannie's tortoise and my little old ivory cross – and soon we were asleep – and who shall say where our spirits wandered? – together, or apart – far in the land of dreams.

And so ends my 6 weeks log – was it worth the time and ink? – who'll say – who'll bother to read it, and having read it, what then? – and who shall I let read it? not many – no not many.

we got these skeleton leaves goin up the side of the track before the sleep before Jacoes!

This leaf is from Jacksons bay 15th.10.90.

from under the old grey stone this little leaf came. Bluff.

This sea fern I picked under the big grey stone we mounted our horses on the Bluff.

This is a bit of the moss fern I was logged in at Jacksons Bay

This Coral moss is off Stewarts Island from up Seal creek what the 2nd mate got.

This leaf is from Jacksons Bay too.

The 2 pansy blossoms dear little old Lizzie brought from "Oaklands"

a bit of that "Lock of Hair"! that "merryanus" sent of the little lass, we left on the Antipodes

from the track in Jacksons Bay.

This leaf I picked under a big grey stone at the Bluff

Epilogue

Lillie

Lillie married Andrew Knox alias "Merryeanus" the ship's carpenter in Wellington several years later. They moved to Kaitawa near Pahiatua to land earlier purchased by Andrew's father. Lillie loved the country life and continued to indulge in her love of horses, which it was said she valued above humans. Lillie and Andrew raised a son Wyndham (named after the southern town) and a daughter Riri (Maori for Lily) on the farm where her granddaughter Cynthia lives today. During the Depression the family left the farm and lived in Pahiatua, but Wyndham returned and developed it into a successful sheep and beef property as soon as his way was clear. Life for the founding families of the Hinemoa Valley, where Kaitawa lies, was one of mutual cooperation and respect and many family connections remain today even though the farms no longer remain in the same ownership.

Ethel

Ethel became a draughtswoman for the Lands and Survey department. She continued to paint in oil and watercolour and sold her paintings both in New Zealand and London. She moved to Waiho, Southland, later in life to be near a married man with whom she was said to be secretly in love. Her paintings were displayed for sale in the Hermitage hotel and many were lost when it was destroyed by fire. During this time she formed a deep platonic relationship with a young mountaineer, Alan Browne, who was some 20 years her junior. She encouraged him to study painting and they maintained a long and enduring friendship. One of her paintings was the medium by which Alan's son and artist Michael Browne was to meet Cynthia in Thorndon, Wellington, a century later. Ethel never married but can be considered an early conservationist because of her efforts to preserve native species and environments.

Fannie

Fannie lived most of her life in Wellington where she continued to paint in watercolour having many works accepted at the Academy of Fine Arts. She was an early illustrator of fauna and flora for the Forest and Bird Society. It seemed that neither she nor Ethel could ever find a man who understood their wild spirits sufficiently to become an acceptable marriage partner. Both Ethel and Fannie shared a somewhat melancholy view of older age and were steadfast in their belief in God. Fannie was a regular visitor to the farm in Kaitawa and is remembered by Cynthia as an enchanting aunt who taught her much about watercolour painting. Cynthia remembers trips to Wellington to shift an elderly Fannie and her numerous parceled-up belongings from one lonely rented single room to another. Fannie kept a treasure trove of family memorabilia and was the source of the material contained in this book.